The Vegetable Garden Displayed

WITH NEARLY
THREE HUNDRED PHOTOGRAPHS

THE ROYAL HORTICULTURAL SOCIETY
VINCENT SQUARE   LONDON SW I

First published 1941
Completely revised 1961
Reprinted with slight revisions 1964
Reprinted with revisions 1966, 1970, 1972

Compiled and published by
THE ROYAL HORTICULTURAL SOCIETY

© 1961 The Royal Horticultural Society

ISBN 0 900629 13 4

Made and Printed in Great Britain
by Jarrold & Sons Ltd, Norwich

contents

The aim of this publication is to provide a simple but authoritative guide to Vegetable Growing for all amateurs, in particular for those who have not done it before. It is not intended as a guide for commercial methods in a market garden, which often differ from those used in the private garden.

NOTE

The majority of these photographs were made in the Society's Garden situated at Wisley, Surrey; it should, therefore, be remembered that the timing of the operations described applies to the south of England. In consequence, they will fall to be done at later dates in the spring in gardens or allotments farther north. Again autumn operations should be carried out at earlier dates in the north than in the south. A gardener must adjust his work to his local conditions of situation and soil; for example, on cold, heavy soils he must not expect to begin so early in the year as he can on the lighter and, therefore, warmer soils, while crops on a northern slope will be a little later to start and will carry on a little longer than those on a southern-facing piece of ground. Cultivars (varieties) listed in seed catalogues now change more frequently and lists are reduced in size, but so far as is possible the cultivars mentioned are believed to be reliable and obtainable. There are of course also good newer cultivars which, as yet, have not been widely tested and are not generally obtainable. The Royal Horticultural Society can accept no liability either for failure to control pests, diseases or weeds by approved or other crop protection products or for damage as a consequence of their use.

ACKNOWLEDGMENT

The help of Mr. J. S. Wolfe and Mr. P. Richardson of the National Institute of Agricultural Engineering in compiling sections on irrigation and machinery is gratefully acknowledged.

THERE ARE MANY forms of false economy in gardening, and the purchase of cheap tools cannot be too strongly condemned. They are inefficient in use, trying to the temper and, of course, expensive in the long run. Buy the best tools you can afford and choose them with care.

A large collection is not necessary, but there are certain essential tools with which the bulk of the work in vegetable gardens may be done.

The spade comes first. Buy one of stainless steel if you can afford to do so. Choose one with the right length of handle to suit yourself. For digging turf, a border spade or chopping spade is useful. The digging equipment will be complete with a four-pronged digging fork. There are many types of hoe; a draw hoe (see p. 7) for taking out drills and a dutch hoe for summer cultivation will be needed. A steel garden rake is necessary, to which may be added a wooden rake for breaking down the ground and clearing up rubbish in the garden. All these tools should be fitted with ash handles.

A good line on a strong iron reel is important, and a wooden measuring rod of 6, 8, or 10 feet. This you can make yourself, marking off every 3 inches by a saw cut.

Among the smaller tools a trowel and a wooden or steel-pointed dibber will be in fairly regular use, and a small hand-hoe, or a hand-fork, is a most useful tool when such jobs as thinning and cleaning beds of seedling onions have to be done. A strong watering-can, with detachable roses of various degrees of coarseness, is a necessity.

There are now many small spraying or dusting machines which are suitable for applying insecticides or fungicides. Equipment used for applying herbicides should be marked accordingly and not used for any other purpose.

It is very important to keep tools clean. They should never be put away with any dirt sticking to them. Scrape as well as possible with a piece of wood, wash the steel and when dry wipe with an oily rag.

To form a really complete equipment, a barrow, if possible with a rubber-tyred wheel, a syringe, a strong knife, a pair of leather gloves and a bundle of plastic or wooden labels will be required.

A few glass or plastic cloches, cold frames or dutch lights, are of real value for raising seedlings for transplanting in the open ground and for the protection of salad crops.

1 Spade.
2 Potato fork, flat prongs.
3 Digging fork.
4 & 5 Garden trowels and hand-forks.
6 Nylon garden line.
7 Steel-pointed dibber.
8 Different hoe-heads.

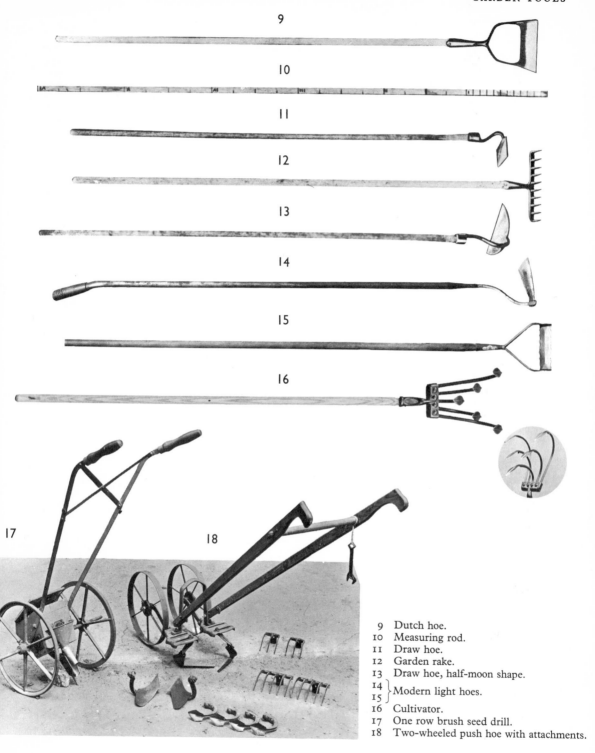

9 Dutch hoe.
10 Measuring rod.
11 Draw hoe.
12 Garden rake.
13 Draw hoe, half-moon shape.
14 ⎱Modern light hoes.
15 ⎰
16 Cultivator.
17 One row brush seed drill.
18 Two-wheeled push hoe with attachments.

how to dig

THERE ARE CERTAIN simple rules which apply to all forms of digging, whether it be digging one spit deep, double digging of cultivated land or double digging of grassland.

In the first place the plot to be dug should be marked off with the aid of a line. Then, as it is necessary to dig out a trench across the width of the plot to be dug in order to facilitate the work, the problem arises of how to dispose of the soil removed from this first trench. If the plot is very small it may be simpler to wheel the soil to the other end of the plot, where it will be ready to fill in the last trench when the work is completed.

On the other hand, if the plot is larger it is a good plan to divide it lengthwise into halves. A line should be stretched down the middle of the plot and with a spade a light furrow may be nicked out along the line. Then the soil should be removed from a trench to a width of 12 inches and the depth of a spade across half the plot at one end. This soil is then deposited at the same end of the plot, but opposite the other half. Digging then proceeds down the first half, and when the end is reached the operator turns round and works back on the second half to finish parallel with the starting-point, and the soil removed from the first trench is ready to fill the last trench.

In the actual operation of digging it should always be remembered that to make a clean and thorough job the spade should be thrust in vertically. If a slanting thrust is used the work not only takes longer but is not dug so deeply.

Then it is always advisable to drive the spade in at right-angles to the trench to cut off the slice of soil that will be lifted next. If each spadeful is not cut off in this way the soil will crack away loosely and a full spadeful cannot be lifted as the soil tends to tumble off the spade.

One word of warning may be given to those who are not accustomed to digging. Do not attempt to do too much to begin with. Half an hour or an hour will be quite sufficient until the muscles are accustomed to the unusual exercise.

DIGGING ONE SPIT DEEP

THIS CONSISTS OF breaking up the soil to the depth of a spade or a fork. The trench is taken out as described above, and the soil from the next strip is turned over into the trench (see pp. 10 and 11).

If manure is to be applied it is a good plan to spread it over the ground to be dug to ensure even distribution, leaving, however, the breadth of the first spade cut clear of manure. When this strip has been dug and the soil removed, the manure from the next strip to the width of a spade should be placed in the trench, laying it on the sloping surface so that while none is left above the surface when the digging is finished it is distributed in the soil from the bottom of the trench almost to the surface. Having put the manure in the trench, the next strip of soil should be turned over into the trench, burying the manure.

DOUBLE DIGGING CULTIVATED GROUND

DIVIDE THE PLOT into two, as described above, and mark out the boundary and dividing lines with a spade; then take out a trench, 2 feet wide, to the depth of the spade and with vertical sides, at the end of one half of the plot. The soil should be placed on the path at the same end of the plot, but opposite the other half, where it will be ready to fill in the last trench. Then break up the bottom of the trench to the full depth of a fork. Take care to break up not only the middle of the bottom of the trench, but also the soil right up to the sides of the trench. Having broken up the bottom of the first trench, a second strip of exactly the same width should be marked off, and for this purpose it is a good plan to keep a stick cut to the right length at each side of the ground which is being trenched. The object in measuring the width of the trenches is to ensure that each time a trench is dug the same quantity of soil is moved. If the same quantity of soil is moved each time it will be easy to keep a level surface. Put the line across at the ends of your sticks to mark how broad the next trench is to be. Then take out the second trench, placing the soil from it on to the broken-up bottom of the first trench. A trench 2 feet wide can be conveniently worked in three spits. Each time the first of the three spits to be moved should be the one farthest from the trench which is being filled in, and it should be placed so that it forms a good wall to the second trench. Then the second and third spits may be moved. The second trench, like the first, should be dug to the full depth of a spade before the bottom is broken up. To do this, it will be necessary to remove the 'crumbs' from the second trench with a spade. When this has been done, the bottom of the second trench is broken up with a fork, the second trench is filled with the soil from the third, and so on (see pp. 12 and 13).

When manure is to be applied in double digging, it should be spread over the broken-up bottom of the trench, and it may be forked into the loose soil there. The manure may be spread over the ground in the same way as for single digging, but each time before a top strip of soil is moved into the trench the manure is transferred to the broken-up bottom of the trench.

DOUBLE DIGGING GRASSLAND

THE PLOT IS divided into two, as described on p. 8, and a trench 2 feet wide is taken out at one end of one half. First of all, the turf is skimmed to a depth of 2 inches, the soil is removed to the depth of a spade and placed, turf and soil separately, opposite the other half of the plot at the same end ready to fill in the last trench. The bottom of the trench is then broken up to the full depth of a fork. The turf from the second strip or trench is skimmed off and placed face downwards on the broken-up bottom of the first trench and chopped up. The top spit of soil from the second trench is then placed on top of the chopped-up turf in the first trench. The 'crumbs' from the second trench are shovelled out with a spade and are thrown on to the surface soil of the first trench. The bottom of the second trench is broken up with a fork. The turf from the third trench is thrown into it, and so on (see p. 14).

1

2

1 First trench 12 inches wide to full depth of spade.
2 Cutting the spit.
3 Placing spade at correct angle.
4 Pressing spade to full depth to insure deep working.

3

4

5

6

5 Lifting full spade of soil.
6 Twisting the spade to reverse soil into trench.
7 Placing a little manure at the bottom of each trench.
8 Spade inserted at wrong angle, resulting in ground not
   being dug deep enough.

7

8

1

2

3

4

5

6

**DOUBLE DIGGING
CULTIVATED GROUND**

1 First trench 2 feet wide full depth of spade.
2 Breaking up second spit to full depth of fork.
3 Marking out second trench 2 feet wide.
4 Transferring soil from second to first trench, working
   from left to right across trench width.
5 Transferring 'crumbs' from second to first trench.
6 Forking bottom of trench before adding manure.
7 Spreading manure.
8 Forking manure into second spit.

8

7

1

2

DOUBLE DIGGING GRASSLAND

1 Preparing first trench—soil removed, breaking up second spit.
2 Placing turf from second trench·upside down in first trench.
3 After chopping turf in first trench covering with soil from second trench, working from left to right across trench width.
4 Transferring 'crumbs' from second to first trench.

3

4

diagram of allotment or garden plots

	MANURED WITH DUNG OR COMPOST	FERTILIZERS AND LIME	FERTILIZERS
PLOT IN THE FIRST YEAR	Section 1 of plot *Peas* *Beans* *Onions* *Leeks* *Lettuces* *Tomatoes* *Spinach* *Spinach Beet* *Celery* SUCCESSION CROPS *Carrots* *Beetroots* *Cabbages*	Section 2 of plot *Cabbages* *Sprouts* *Cauliflowers* *Kales* *Broccoli* *Seed-bed for* *Green crops* SUCCESSION CROPS *Onions*	Section 3 of plot *Potatoes* *Carrots* *Beetroots* *Parsnips* *Swedes* SUCCESSION CROPS *Spinach* *Lettuces*
	FERTILIZERS AND LIME	**FERTILIZERS**	**MANURED WITH DUNG OR COMPOST**
PLOT IN THE SECOND YEAR	Section 1 of plot *Cabbages* *Sprouts* *Cauliflowers* *Kales* *Broccoli* *Seed-bed for* *Green crops* SUCCESSION CROPS *Onions*	Section 2 of plot *Potatoes* *Carrots* *Beetroots* *Parsnips* *Swedes* SUCCESSION CROPS *Spinach* *Lettuces*	Section 3 of plot *Peas* *Beans* *Onions* *Leeks* *Lettuces* *Tomatoes* *Spinach* *Spinach Beet* *Celery* SUCCESSION CROPS *Carrots* *Beetroots* *Cabbages*
	FERTILIZERS	**MANURED WITH DUNG OR COMPOST**	**FERTILIZERS AND LIME**
PLOT IN THE THIRD YEAR	Section 1 of plot *Potatoes* *Carrots* *Beetroots* *Parsnips* *Swedes* SUCCESSION CROPS *Spinach* *Lettuces*	Section 2 of plot *Peas* *Beans* *Onions* *Leeks* *Lettuces* *Tomatoes* *Spinach* *Spinach Beet* *Celery* SUCCESSION CROPS *Carrots* *Beetroots* *Cabbages*	Section 3 of plot *Cabbages* *Sprouts* *Cauliflowers* *Kales* *Broccoli* *Seed-bed for* *Green crops* SUCCESSION CROPS *Onions*

cropping plan for garden or allotment

INCHES	MAIN CROP	SUCCESSION CROP	CATCH CROP
24	RUNNER BEANS, double row, sow half row mid-May, half mid-June	CABBAGES, three rows, plant in September	
12	SHALLOTS, plant February		
36	ONIONS (August sown), plant three rows in March		
36	ONIONS, sow three rows early March		
12	SPINACH, sow half rows end February, end March	LETTUCES, sow half rows mid-May and early June	
12	LETTUCES, sow half rows early and mid-April	LETTUCES, sow half rows late June and early July	
27	BROAD BEANS, double row, sow half end February, and half end March	CARROTS, four rows, sow July	
60	PEAS, sow one row early March and one row early April	BEETROOTS (round), two rows, sow July	
60	LEEKS, four rows, plant July		RADISHES, sow half rows early and late March / LETTUCES, sow half rows mid- and late March
15	SPINACH BEET, sow July		
15	TOMATOES, plant early June		LETTUCES, sow early May
48	DWARF BEANS, one row, sow half row early May and half row late May / CELERY, trench / MARROWS		

INCHES	MAIN CROP	SUCCESSION CROP	CATCH CROP
54	CABBAGES, three rows, planted previous September		ONIONS (white for spring salad), sow July / ONIONS for transplanting, sow August
18	CABBAGES (summer), plant early June		
24	CAULIFLOWERS (autumn), plant July		TURNIPS, half rows, sow early April and May
24	BROCCOLI (winter cauliflower), plant July		BRUSSELS SPROUTS, sow mid-March
24	CABBAGES (winter), plant in July		ONIONS (white for salads), sow March
48	SAVOYS (late), two rows, plant in July		KALE (Cottager's), half row, sow mid-May / CABBAGES (winter), half row, SAVOYS (late), half row, sow early May
81	BRUSSELS SPROUTS, three rows, plant early June		
24	KALE (Cottager's), plant late July		CAULIFLOWERS (autumn), half row, BROCCOLI (winter cauliflower), half row, sow end of April / BROCCOLI (late Purple Sprouting), half row, sow early April / CABBAGES (summer), half row, sow early April
24	BROCCOLI (late Purple Sprouting), plant late July	COMPOST HEAP	LEEKS, sow mid-March
18	KALE (Hungry Gap), sow mid-July		
18	TURNIPS (for tops), sow end August		

[17]

SECTION 3

INCHES	MAIN CROP	SUCCESSION CROP	CATCH CROP
162	POTATOES (main crop), six rows, plant late April	WINTER SPINACH, sow September LETTUCES (winter), sow September	
48	POTATOES (early), two rows, plant early April	CABBAGES for transplanting, sow in July or early August TURNIPS, two rows, sow late July	
21	BEETROOTS (round), sow April		
36	CARROTS (early), sow March CARROTS (main crop), two rows, sow June		
36	GARDEN SWEDES, two rows, sow June		
54	PARSNIPS, three rows, sow March or May		

These plots are not drawn to scale. The total dimensions of the whole area, which is divided into three plots, are 90 feet × 30 feet.

explanation of the cropping plan

THE CROPPING PLAN on the previous pages (15–18) shows the lay-out of an allotment plot or beds in a garden, designed to provide a succession of vegetables throughout the year and to utilize the full capacity of the ground by suitable succession and catch crops.

In order to provide for a rotation the ground is divided into three sections; it will be seen that any given group of vegetables rarely comes on the same land until after an interval of two years. This prevents the carry-over of certain pests and diseases and also provides for the better utilization of the tillage and manuring as some crops respond to fresh manure while others prefer land that has been manured for a previous crop. Again by this system of grouping the crops it is possible to clear the greater part of one section in time to permit of deep digging and the application of dung or compost during the winter and early spring, a treatment which need not be repeated until the rotation has been completed. On this freshly-manured section 1, the beans, leeks, lettuces, onions and peas are sown, as these crops require the richest ground that can be given to them. Some of these crops will be cleared in time to allow succession or catch crops to be sown which will still give some produce during the year.

The second section which follows carries the green crops that are ready from late summer and carry on to provide green vegetables throughout the winter and into the spring until the first of the new season's crops are ready. These Brassica crops are usually raised on seed beds and transplanted; but provision is made for raising the young plants in rows between the places where the crop will be transplanted later.

The third section which completes the rotation, is mainly devoted to the all-important root crops – beetroots, carrots, parsnips and potatoes. If this section has been in cultivation as recommended in previous years it will require little further treatment, though a dressing of fertilizers (see p. 20) is to be recommended. The ground on this section which will carry the root crops should be dug one full spit deep.

It will be noticed that the plan provides for various succession crops which follow as soon as the land can be cleared of the crop first sown. Some of these, like lettuces, onions for pulling green, radishes, etc., only occupy the land for a short time. Others are started in the autumn to carry on through the winter and mature in the following season. It is recommended to make several successive sowings of beetroots and carrots to be pulled young for use in the summer; these catch crops are in addition to the main sowings which are to provide mature roots for storage and winter use. Further information on Succession Crops will be found on p. 99.

It should be noted that the plan is designed for gardens in the south of England; the dates of sowing and harvesting will require to be modified by gardeners in more northern situations. The northern gardener will probably omit broccoli, tomatoes and in many cases also runner beans, replacing them by summer cabbages and cauliflowers. The plan indeed provides for a greater variety of crops than many gardeners and allotment-holders will require, especially those who are making a beginning on newly broken land. It is important to remember that all plans can be no more than suggestions; every gardener has to make adjustments to suit his soil, situation and climate as well as the personal tastes of himself and his family. In substituting other crops for those on the plan, care should be taken to avoid a glut in summer or a scarcity at other times of the year, especially the months from February to May. Any extra ground above the family requirements should be given up to carrots, potatoes or other roots which can be stored and will always be welcome to the growers' friends.

MANURES AND FERTILIZERS

DIVIDE YOUR GARDEN or allotment into three equal pieces for the rotation of your crops—(1) beans, leeks, onions and peas; (2) green crops; (3) potatoes and roots. Keep all the stable manure and the compost heap for the piece on which you are going to grow the beans, leeks, onions and peas. Dig in manure, garden compost or horticultural peat during the winter as early as you can.

The correct use of fertilizers presents rather a problem to the beginner—there are many little doubtful points that arise; what are the best fertilizers, when should they be applied, in what quantity, and so on. As a beginning, we must grasp the fact that all growing crops require from the ground supplies of nitrogen, potash, and phosphoric acid. These nutrients are obtainable in different forms—e.g., the nitrogenous fertilizers include sulphate of ammonia and nitrate of soda; potash is usually supplied in the form of sulphate of potash and muriate of potash; and the phosphoric acid is most commonly applied in the form of bone meal or superphosphate. Fertilizers should be applied when supplies of farmyard manure or garden compost are scarce, and even when they are obtainable it is wise to supplement them with applications of fertilizers. As the valuable constituents of some of these fertilizers are easily washed down into the soil by rain, most of them are usually applied 10 to 14 days before sowing or planting, and hoed or forked lightly into the surface of the soil.

The chief fertilizers you will want are sulphate of ammonia or nitrate of soda, bone meal or superphosphate and sulphate of potash or muriate of potash. On heavy soils, basic slag can be used in place of superphosphate. Sulphate of potash or muriate of potash are particularly valuable for sandy or gravel soils. Wood ashes contain potash and should be carefully collected and stored in a dry place. You will need for all purposes about 2 lb. of sulphate of ammonia, 5 lb. of superphosphate and 2 lb. of sulphate of potash for every square rod (30½ square yards) you are going to crop. This means 20 lb. of sulphate of ammonia, 50 lb. of superphosphate, and 20 lb. of sulphate of potash for an ordinary allotment of 10 rods.

Fertilizers such as sulphate of ammonia or nitrate of soda, which are especially valuable for green crops, are usually applied either 10 to 14 days before planting time or during the growing period of the plants. Nitrate of potash is a fertilizer containing both nitrogen and potash and is very suitable for top dressing all the brassica crops, celery, lettuces and spinach, during the growing season. General or compound fertilizers which contain nitrogen, phosphoric acid and potash can also be used for all vegetables; fertilizers of this type are best applied at the rate of 5 lb. per square rod about a fortnight before sowing or planting. There are a number of proprietary liquid fertilizers which can be applied during the growing season.

Now, how should these fertilizers be used? This will depend, of course, upon whether your ground is newly broken-up grassland, ground previously cultivated but which has received no manure, or ground which has been manured all over or in part.

Grassland broken up for the first time will probably not need a great deal of sulphate of ammonia or nitrate of soda for the first two or three years, but the part where you intend to grow your green and root vegetables should be dressed with 5 lb. of super-phosphate and 2 lb. of sulphate of potash per square rod a fortnight before planting or sowing.

Gardens or plots previously cultivated, but which have received no manure since the previous crop, should be dressed with 5 lb. of bone meal or superphosphate per square rod, mixed with 2 lb. of sulphate of potash per square rod. This should be done when the ground is clear of crops and before sowing or planting begins. Sulphate of ammonia and nitrate of soda may be given to the growing crops as they require it, at the rate of 2 lb. per square rod, or half that quantity of sulphate of ammonia may be mixed with the other fertilizers and applied before sowing or planting and half kept to dress the growing crops later.

If you manured part of your plot—that is, the part reserved for beans, leeks, onions and peas—the whole of the unmanured part should be dressed with a mixture of 2 lb. of sulphate of potash and 5 lb. of superphosphate per square rod before sowing or planting; and 2 lb. of sulphate of ammonia or nitrate of soda should be applied during the growing season to the crops, should they require it. The manured part could be given a light dressing of about 1 lb. of sulphate of potash, mixed with $2\frac{1}{2}$ lb. of bone meal or superphosphate per square rod, to supplement its fertility. If you have manured the whole plot, you could give it the light dressing recommended above. Allotment-holders should club together to buy these fertilizers, for they are much cheaper when they can be bought by the ton. Fertilizers must be stored under shelter and the bags should be kept off the ground.

Most gardens need lime from time to time, usually about once every three years. Lime may be supplied as ground chalk, limestone or hydrated lime. The best plan is to lime one-third of the vegetable garden every year, usually the piece that has been dug for the brassica or green crops. Apply 15 lb. of ground chalk or limestone or 10 lb. of hydrated lime to the surface of each square rod after digging has been completed. One square rod$=30\frac{1}{2}$ square yards.

THE COMPOST HEAP

MARK OUT A PLOT of level ground about 9 feet by 4 feet. Put all waste vegetable matter on to this in the form of a layer—weeds, outside leaves of cabbages, broccoli, lettuces, pea haulms, soft hedge-clippings, lawn-mowings, waste straw, and dead leaves in the autumn, but keep out thick stuff like cabbage-stalks. Diseased plant material should not be put on the heap. If you can get any animal manure spread that on top of the rubbish to make a second layer. Tread from time to time. If no manure is available, sprinkle the heap with sulphate of ammonia at the rate of $\frac{1}{2}$ oz. to the square yard—i.e., 2 oz. for a 9 feet by 4 feet plot. Sprinkle the heap with 8 gallons of water. Proprietary products are obtainable which may be used in place of the sulphate of ammonia. Throw soil about an inch thick over the whole (see pp. 22 and 23).

When you have more rubbish build up another layer on the top, and apply ground chalk or limestone at 4 oz. per square yard. This is followed by watering and another layer of soil.

Go on building up layer after layer applying the manure or sulphate of ammonia and lime to each alternate layer until the heap is about 4 feet high. After that it is better to begin another heap.

In dry summer weather water every week. Turn the heap right over after a month in summer weather and water again if it is dry. In cool weather and in the autumn it may not be ready to turn until after six weeks. After turning, top up with soil and leave it until you are ready to dig it in.

1

2

THE COMPOST HEAP

1 Starting the heap with waste vegetable material.
2 Treading the heap.
3 Adding sulphate of ammonia.
4 Adding layer of waste material—lawn mowings, etc.

3

4

5

6

5 Adding a sprinkling of ground chalk.
6 Watering to keep heap moist.
7 Heap completed.
8 Heap rotted down and compost ready for use.

7

8

SEED SOWING, THINNING AND TRANSPLANTING

THE CULTIVARS (VARIETIES) MENTIONED in this book are believed to be reliable and obtainable; in many cases there are good newer cultivars (varieties) which as yet have not been so widely tested.

For sowing, choose a spell of fine weather when the soil is dry enough to allow treading without soil adhering to the boots. Hoe or lightly fork over the ground to a depth of 2 or 3 inches to allow the soil to dry until it will crumble to a fine tilth, which is the most important feature of a seed bed. When the soil is in this state, it should be firmed by treading with the feet, and then raked over to provide a fine tilth and to remove large stones and rough clods. Then mark out the position of the rows; wherever possible the rows should run from north to south, or north-east to south-west where strong winds may be expected. Stretch a line where the row is to come and take out a drill with a draw-hoe to a depth suited to the seeds to be sown. Always remember to sow thinly. In the case of vegetables which can be transplanted successfully, e.g. beans and peas, it is a good plan to sow a small clump at the end of the row from which gaps can be repaired. In continued dry weather the ground in which the seeds are to be sown should be thoroughly watered the day before sowing.

Begin to thin early, as soon as the plants are fit to handle, but thin in successive stages so as to avoid complete failures in case of losses caused by pests and diseases. Gaps can be filled up by transplanting either from the thinnings or the surplus sowing made at the ends of the row, but it should be remembered that tap-rooted plants, like beetroots and carrots, can rarely be transplanted with success. In dry weather thinning should be done in the evening and the bed should be watered afterwards.

Most of the *Brassica* crops and leeks can best be raised on small nursery seed beds, and the seedlings transplanted later into the cropping positions. The seed bed should be well cultivated and brought to a fine tilth. The rows should be 6 inches apart, and the seedlings should be carefully thinned in their early stages until they are at least an inch apart. The bed should be thoroughly soaked with water the night before the seedlings are transplanted. Planting should be done before the plants become hard or drawn. Lift the plants with a fork or hand-fork and protect from the sun or drying wind until they have been moved to their fresh situation. The bed in which the young plants are to grow should be made firm before drawing drills, about 2 inches deep. In dry weather the drill should be watered the night before transplanting. Planting out may be done by either a dibber or a trowel. The seedlings should be firmly planted, taking care to avoid leaving a cavity under the roots. After transplanting give the plants a thorough watering (see pp. 25–27).

The sowing and planting distances which follow have been thoroughly tested but there is now a tendency, supported by scientific investigation, to sow and plant vegetables more closely.

1 Firming the prepared ground by treading.
2 Raking to obtain fine tilth.
3 Drawing shallow drills 6 inches apart with short stick, footboard used to protect seed bed.
4 Sowing seeds.

1

3

SEED-BED AND SEED SOWING

1 Firming prepared ground by treading.
2 Raking to obtain fine tilth.
3 Measuring rod and marking pegs.
4 Setting out position of rows.

2

4

5

6

5 Drawing drills 12 inches apart, 1 inch deep, suitable for
  parsnips.
6 Sowing seeds.
7 Covering seeds.
8 Raking over the sown bed.

7

8

potatoes

TRUSTWORTHY CULTIVARS (VARIETIES). Earlies: Foremost, Home Guard and Ulster Chieftain. Maincrop: Dr. McIntosh, King Edward (susceptible to wart disease), Majestic, Pentland Crown and Pentland Dell.

PREPARATION OF THE GROUND. Potatoes may be grown on newly broken pasture land provided precautions have been taken against wireworm. Manure should be applied unless that part of the garden or allotment was manured in the previous season. In either case the land should be dressed at planting time with 2 lb. of mixed fertilizer (1 part of sulphate of ammonia, 2 parts of superphosphate and 1 part of sulphate potash) to the row of 30 feet. If the pasture has been in good heart the sulphate of ammonia may be omitted. Dig the ground during winter and leave it rough until planting time. If the growth is not satisfactory the land may be dressed with 1 lb. of sulphate of ammonia per 30 yard row and hoed in just before earthing up.

PLANTING. Tubers weighing 2 to 3 oz. (the size of a large egg) makes the best 'seed'. When larger, cut lengthwise (see p. 29) at planting time. Certain varieties, such as Majestic, heal the cut surface slowly and it is advisable to plant this variety in moist soil as soon as possible after cutting. Place the potato tubers in trays in a light, airy, frost-proof place in February to sprout (see p. 29). During early April plant the sprouted tubers in drills 4 to 5 inches deep taken out with a draw-hoe or spade. The early cultivars should be 12 inches apart, in rows 24 inches apart. Tubers of the late cultivars should be planted 15 inches apart, in rows 27 inches apart during late April (see pp. 30 and 31).

CULTIVATION. If necessary, protect the young growths of early potatoes from late frosts, either by drawing a little soil up over them with a hoe or covering them with protective material, such as bracken or straw. Before earthing, hoe between the rows to destroy seedling weeds. Earth up the plants with a hoe as growth proceeds, but not higher than 6 inches. Spray, as recommended below, against potato blight (see p. 33).

HARVESTING AND STORING. Lift the early crops as required when they are ready, usually in July or early August, and the later varieties in September or early October for storing. Exercise care in lifting them. Potatoes intended to be stored should be allowed to dry on the surface of the soil for two or three hours before storing in clamps in the open or in boxes in a frost-proof shed (see pp. 34 and 35). Potatoes should always be stored in the dark to prevent them becoming green.

PESTS AND DISEASES. Many pests attack this crop, but wireworms cause the greatest havoc, especially in freshly converted pasture and waste land. Grow early cultivars where damage is expected and lift the maincrop cultivars as soon as the tubers are mature. Slugs may be discouraged by limiting the use of organic manures on heavier soils, by cultivating thoroughly and by using baits based on methiocarb (Draza) or metaldehyde. Metaldehyde may also be applied as a spray. On freshly broken ground grow only early or mid-season varieties, and lift the crop by mid-August. Potato cyst eelworm is a serious pest where potatoes are grown too frequently on the same site. There is no effective chemical treatment available but strict adherence to an adequate rotation will usually prevent trouble.

Spray the maincrop varieties in early July with maneb, zineb or Bordeaux mixture as a preventive against blight. Tubers which have become infected should not be stored. If the disease appears at the end of the season on the dying tops, cut them off and burn

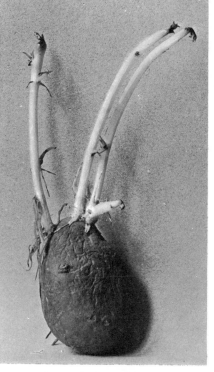

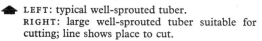 LEFT: typical well-sprouted tuber.
RIGHT: large well-sprouted tuber suitable for cutting; line shows place to cut.

Badly sprouted tuber; spindly sprouts due to being kept in too dark or too warm a place.

A convenient type of box filled with well-sprouted tubers.

them to avoid tuber infection. Scab on the skin is generally due to lack of humus in the soil and to counteract this dig in manure, vegetable compost or even grass-mowings. In case of wart disease plant only *immune* varieties.

[29]

1

2

1 Drawing drills 4 to 5 inches deep with large draw hoe.
2 Planting tubers 12 or 15 inches apart, in drill.
3 Covering tubers lightly with soil prior to applying fertilizers.
4 Sulphate of ammonia, superphosphate and sulphate of potash ready for mixing.

3

4

5

6

5 Mixing fertilizers.
6 Applying fertilizers at rate of 2 lb. to row 30 feet long.
7 Filling in and slightly mounding over drills.
8 Forking between rows, leaving slight mounding.

7

8

1

2

POTATO EARTHING

1 Cleaning ground prior to earthing.
2 Earthing up the rows: straddling the row.
3 Earthing up the rows: standing between two rows.
4 Earthing completed, leaving ground free of all footmarks.

4

3

1

2

POTATO SPRAYING

1 Mixing up Bordeaux mixture spray.
2 Pneumatic sprayer in operation.
3 Continuous bucket sprayer in use.
4 Applying spray with a fine rose
   watering-can.

3

4

1

2

POTATO LIFTING

1 Lifting root clear of ground before shaking off tubers.
2 Lifted plant, showing tubers attached.
3 Crop lifted: haulms removed: potatoes laid out to dry
   for 2 to 3 hours before storing.
4 Crop graded: 'ware or eating'; 'seed'; 'chats'.

3

4

POTATO CLAMPING

1 Laying straw over prepared bottom of clamp.

2 Potatoes heaped in position on straw bottom.

3 Straw covering.

4 Section of clamp showing earthing and ridge left open to allow for sweating.

5 Clamp completely enclosed after allowing a period for sweating.

[35]

carrots

TRUSTWORTHY CULTIVARS. Long Pointed Cultivar: New Red Intermediate. Other than a Long Pointed Cultivar: Amsterdam Forcing, Nantes, Favourite, Autumn King.

PREPARATION OF THE GROUND. Leave the surface rough until sowing time, then break it down to a fine tilth.

SEED SOWING. Make the first sowing in March in rows 9 to 12 inches apart, covering the seeds to a depth of $\frac{3}{4}$ inch. Make monthly sowings at intervals until the end of July, according to needs. Broadcast seed very thinly when sowing in frames or cloches.

CULTIVATION. Hoe between the rows and thin the seedlings when the first rough leaf appears. Thin again twice until the final distance between the plants is 2 inches for stump-rooted varieties and 4 inches for intermediate or long varieties. The thinnings from the latter should be used for the kitchen. To minimize the risk of attack from the carrot fly, thin only on dull days or after sunset and water the rows thoroughly after thinning.

HARVESTING AND STORING. Pull the early sowings as required as soon as they are large enough for eating. The roots for storage should be lifted in October with a fork; reject any diseased or pest-infested roots, twist off the tops and remove the soil from the roots. Be careful not to bruise or damage the roots. Store either in boxes of sand or soil in a frost-proof shed; against the inside wall of a similar building; or in a clamp in the open (see p. 40). The last sowings can be left in the ground until much later; in favoured localities they need not be lifted until wanted, provided they are covered with a little strawy material or bracken when severe frost threatens.

PESTS. The carrot fly is the most destructive pest, especially in light soils. Where possible sow in exposed positions and sow thinly to reduce the need for singling since the odour of crushed foliage attracts the flies. Apply lindane seed dressing at $\frac{2}{3}$ to 1 oz. of gamma-BHC/1 lb. of seed. If this dosage is exceeded tainting may occur. Alternatively, apply soil drenches of trichlorphon in May and June on early carrots and in July and August on maincrop.

1 Early Gem.
2 Amsterdam Forcing.
3 Nantes.
4 Chantenay Red-Cored.
5 Autumn King.
6 St. Valery.

CARROT SOWING

1 Applying a good general fertilizer.
2 Drawing drills 12 inches apart, $\frac{3}{4}$ inch deep.
3 Sowing seeds.
4 Covering the seeds.

1

2

3

4

1

2

CARROT THINNING

1 Rows of seedlings ready for thinning.
2 First thinning to 1 inch apart.
3 Carrot Amsterdam Forcing sown broadcast under Dutch lights.
   Little thinning required.

3

1

2

3

CARROT HARVESTING

1   Pulling roots by hand for immediate use.

2   Lifting roots with fork for storing.

3   Cutting off tops prior to storing.

[39]

1

2

CARROT STORING

1 Carrots heaped for clamping outdoors.
2 Straw covering in position.
3 Heap covered with soil.
4 Carrots heaped for storing in sand in a shed.

3

4

BEETROOTS

TRUSTWORTHY CULTIVARS. Round: Boltardy, Early Bunch (suitable for sowing in March), Crimson Globe, Detroit Red (suitable for sowing in April). Intermediate: Cylindra. Long: Cheltenham Green Top.

PREPARATION OF THE GROUND. Beetroots should not be sown on freshly manured ground. If the land is in poor heart, a little fertilizer may be given before sowing, as described in the section on manures and fertilizers.

SOWING. Sow in drills in March and April one row of a round type to provide early roots to pull in the summer. Make the main sowing from the middle of May to early June of the long type for storage. When more than one row is sown, the rows should be 12 inches apart and 1 inch deep. A late sowing of the round type may be made in July to be pulled for use in late winter (see p. 102).

CULTIVATION. Hoe between the rows and when the first rough leaf appears thin the seedlings to 2 inches. Thin again until the final distance between the plants is 4 inches, making sure that only a single plant is left in each place.

HARVESTING AND STORING. Pull the early sowings as required as soon as they are large enough for eating. The roots for storage should be lifted with a fork in October; reject any damaged or pest-infested roots, twist off the tops and shake the soil from the roots. Be careful not to bruise or damage the roots. Store either in boxes of sand or peat in a frost-proof shed, against the inside wall of a similar building, or in a clamp in the open (see p. 45). The last sowings can be left in the ground until much later; in favoured localities they need not be lifted until wanted, provided they are covered with a little strawy material or bracken where severe frost threatens.

PARSNIPS

TRUSTWORTHY CULTIVARS. Short: Avonresister, Offenham. Intermediate: Hollow Crown. Long: Lisbonnais, Tender and True.

PREPARATION OF THE GROUND. Grow parsnips on ground that was manured for a previous crop (see Plan, p. 15). Dig deeply and leave rough until seed-sowing time. Then work down to a fine tilth. On soils unsuitable for deep-rooted crops sow seeds of Offenham or prepare special places for the plants (see pp. 42 and 43).

SEED SOWING. Seeds can either be sown at the first opportunity during the month of March when the condition of the soil is suitable, or later during May, in drills 12 inches apart (see p. 27).

CULTIVATION. When the seedlings have germinated and are large enough to handle, thin them, leaving the plants 6 inches apart. Hoe regularly.

HARVESTING. Parsnips are usually left in the ground until required for use, but it is advisable to lift the remaining roots early in March and store them by burying them in soil or sand in a shed or outhouse to check them from starting into growth.

PESTS. The chief enemy is the celery fly or leaf-miner (see celery, p. 78).

1

[42]

3

PARSNIPS

1 Making holes 10 to 12 inches apart in soils unsuitable
for deep-rooted crops.
2 Filling in holes with sifted soil to within 1 inch of the
surface.
3 Sowing 4 to 5 seeds in each hole.
4 Covering seeds with sifted soil.

2

4

5

6

PARSNIPS

5 First thinning leaving two plants.
6 Plants ready for second thinning.
7 Second and final thinning.
8 Lifting roots as required for use.

[43]

7

8

3

4

1

2

BEETROOTS

1 Sowing on prepared ground in drills 12 inches apart and 1 inch deep.
2 First thinning 2 inches apart.
3 Second and final thinning, 4 inches apart.
4 Lifting roots for immediate use.

1

2

STORING BEETROOTS

1 Lifting long beetroots with fork.
2 Twisting off leaves not too close to crown.
3 Storing a small quantity of round beetroots in sand.
4 Storing beetroots in sand in a shed.

[45]

3

4

turnips and garden swedes

TURNIPS

TRUSTWORTHY CULTIVARS. Early, flat-round roots: Purple Milan, White Milan. Early, round roots: Snowball. Maincrop, round roots: Golden Ball, Green-Top Stone.

PREPARATION OF THE GROUND. For early cultivars dig a piece of ground that was manured in the previous season and dress it with 3 oz. of a general fertilizer to the square yard. For late varieties choose ground that has been cleared of an early crop. Lightly cultivate and hoe in a dressing of 3 oz. of a general fertilizer per square yard.

SEED SOWING. Make a first sowing of an early cultivar in early April in drills $\frac{3}{4}$ inch deep and 15 inches apart. Follow with successional sowings at intervals of about three weeks until early July. Sow the late cultivars for storage in late July. For turnip tops sow thinly the cultivar Green-Top Stone at the end of August in rows 9 to 12 inches apart and do not thin.

CULTIVATION. Begin thinning the seedlings when the first rough leaves appear. Continue to thin in stages until the plants are 6 inches apart. Hoe regularly.

HARVESTING AND STORING. Pull the early cultivars for use while they are young. In autumn lift carefully with a fork those intended for storing; avoid damaging or bruising them. Reject any diseased or pest-infested roots, twist off the tops and store in boxes of sand or soil in a dry, frost-proof shed. Alternatively store in clamps in the open as advised for carrots (see p. 40).

PESTS. Flea-beetles or turnip fly attack the seed-leaves of turnips. This pest is only serious in dry weather, and can be checked by watering the seedlings every evening after sunset until the plants are growing freely. Spray or dust the seedlings with BHC, repeating at weekly intervals until the rough leaves appear.

GARDEN SWEDES

TRUSTWORTHY CULTIVAR. Any purple-topped cultivar.

PREPARATION OF THE GROUND. See turnips.

SEED SOWING. Sow in drills 15 to 18 inches apart, $\frac{3}{4}$ inch deep, about mid-June.

CULTIVATION. See turnips. Thin to 1 foot apart.

HARVESTING AND STORING. See turnips.

PESTS. See turnips.

DISEASES. Do not forget that swedes can suffer severely from club root disease and the land may need treatment by liming, as given under cabbages (see p. 69).

1

2

TURNIPS

1 Sowing on prepared ground, in drills 15 inches apart, $\frac{3}{4}$ inch deep.
2 First thinning, 3 inches apart.
3 Second and final thinning, 6 inches apart.
4 Pulling roots as required for use.

[47]

3

4

onions

TRUSTWORTHY CULTIVARS. January sown under glass and planted in the open: Ailsa Craig, Lancastrian. Spring-sown: Bedfordshire Champion, Best of All (Up-to-Date), Giant Zittau. August-sown: Reliance, Solidity. Salad: White Lisbon. Sets: Rijnsburger, Stuttgarter Riesen.

PREPARATION OF THE GROUND. Dig thoroughly and deeply during the winter, working in any farmyard manure or compost obtainable. Leave the land in ridges to allow the frost to work upon it. Break down the ridges in February as soon as the land is dry enough. Cultivate to a light tilth. When the soil is dry enough not to pick up on the boot, tread firmly before sowing or transplanting (see p. 49).

JANUARY SOWING UNDER GLASS. Onion seeds can be sown under glass in January and the seedlings transplanted instead of sowing outside; the cultivar Ailsa Craig is particularly suitable for this purpose. If you have no greenhouse, use cloches or frames. Transplant about the middle of April when conditions are favourable, and the seedlings are thoroughly hardened, setting out the plants in rows 12 to 15 inches apart and 6 to 8 inches between the plants. Plant with a trowel and take care to keep their base about a $\frac{1}{4}$ inch below ground and allow the roots their full depth (see p. 51).

SPRING SOWING. On the first favourable occasion between mid-February and the end of March, sow in drills, 12 inches apart. Just cover the seeds with soil and firm the surface (see p. 50).

AUTUMN SOWING. Sow in drills in August, at the beginning of the month in the north, later in the south. Plant out in early March in rows 12 to 15 inches apart and 6 to 8 inches between the plants. Later operations are the same as for spring sowing.

ONION SETS. Do not apply manure for this crop, but the ground should be dressed with 3 oz. of superphosphate and 1 oz. of sulphate of potash per square yard, 10 to 14 days before planting. Plant in early April in shallow drills 12 inches apart, placing the sets 6 inches apart in the row. Cover the sets with soil to leave only the necks exposed. Later operations are the same as for spring sowing, although crops grown from onion sets are often easier to grow and harvest, particularly in the northern or wetter parts of the country.

CULTIVATION. Hoe and hand-weed as soon as onions sown in the open ground are visible. Make a first thinning when the onions are 2 inches high, leaving the plants about an inch apart. Continue to hoe and weed and make two thinnings altogether so that, in the end, the single plants are 4 inches apart. Use the second thinnings for salads.

HARVESTING. About mid-August or a little later, bend the tops over to hasten the ripening of the bulbs. A fortnight later lift the bulbs carefully and ripen off in a dry, sunny place (see p. 52).

STORAGE. When dry make up the onions into ropes or bunches and hang them in a dry airy place, as under the rafters of a shed. Alternatively, store in trays with a slatted or netting bottom. If severe weather threatens, protect them from frost (see p. 53).

PESTS AND DISEASES. The most serious trouble comes from the onion fly. It is most troublesome on dry soils. Attacked plants should be dug up whole and burned. Ensure that no larvae are left in the soil around the roots. When sowing sprinkle lindane dust in the seed drills or apply a 4-inch band along the rows at the loop stage and again 10 days later. Onions may be tainted by this treatment. A possible alternative is to water a solution of trichlorphon on to the soil about the end of May, repeating twice at 10-day intervals. Mildew appears as grey or purplish spots or streaks on the leaves and at the first sign of this dust the plants when moist with copper lime dust (Bordeaux powder) or spray with zineb. White rot, which affects the roots and base of the bulb resulting in yellowing of the leaves, can be prevented by growing onions on a different site each year, or by applying 4% calomel dust at the rate of 1 lb. to each 25 yards of drill at the time of sowing. Neck-rot disease often destroys many onions in store and it is important to dry the bulbs after lifting, if necessary under cover to avoid them remaining damp for any length of time. Infestation of plants by onion eelworm causes swelling and distortion of the tissues producing symptoms commonly referred to as "bloat". Eelworms can be carried in the seed and if any part of the garden becomes infested it is best to refrain from growing onions on or near the affected area for at least three years. No suitable chemical treatment is available.

ONIONS—PREPARATION OF THE GROUND

1 Applying a good general fertilizer.
2 Firming the ground by treading.

3 Raking to obtain a fine tilth.
4 Drawing drills 12 inches apart and ¾ inch deep.

1

2

ONION SOWING AND THINNING

1 Sowing seeds in drills 12 inches apart, $\frac{3}{4}$ inch deep.
2 Covering the seeds.
3 First thinning to 1 inch apart.
4 Second and final thinning 4 inches apart.

3

4

1

2

ONION PLANTING

1 Pricking out seedlings raised under glass.
2 Box of seedling onions ready for planting out.
3 Planting out in rows 12 inches apart, plants 6 inches apart.
4 Bed of onions in summer growth.

3

4

1

2

ONION SETS

1 Planting onion sets 6 inches apart in shallow drills
    spaced 1 foot apart.

HARVESTING

2 Tops bent over to hasten ripening.
3 Onions lifted and laid with roots facing sun.
4 Crop laid on wire frame for drying.

3

4

1

2

ONION STORING

1 Making an onion rope.
2 Tying onions on to the rope.
3 Rope completed.
4 Ropes stored in shed.

[53]

3

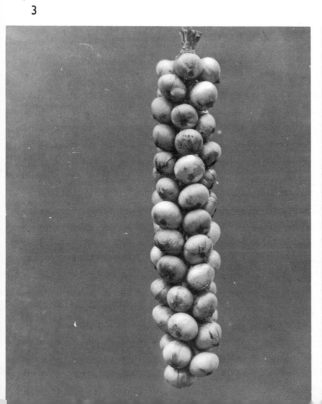

4

leeks, shallots

LEEKS

TRUSTWORTHY CULTIVARS.   Early use: Prizetaker. Maincrop: Musselburgh. Late: Royal Favourite.

PREPARATION OF THE GROUND.   Leeks repay the trouble of thorough digging, although they are not so exacting in their requirements as onions. If you are not going to plant on the land manured in the winter (see p. 19), dig in manure or compost when turning the ground over after the previous crop is cleared.

SEED SOWING.   Leeks may be sown from late February to early March until mid-April on a small prepared seed-bed (see p. 25), according to the weather and state of the ground. Early sowing will produce a large leek for transplanting which is an advantage.

TRANSPLANTING.   If the soil is dry, soak the seed-bed previous to lifting. Lift the seedlings carefully with a fork when they are about 8 inches high and trim the leaves slightly. Set them out 9 inches apart in rows 15 inches apart. Make a hole with the dibber and place the young plant in it. Do not fill the hole—a watering when planting is completed will tighten the plants sufficiently. An alternative method is to draw out drills 4 inches deep and 15 inches apart. Plant with 9 inches between the plants.

CULTIVATION.   Hoe regularly to aerate the soil and to keep down weeds. Draw a little soil up to the stems of leeks, if planted in drills, just before they are fully grown. Leeks are among the hardiest of vegetables and may be left in the ground until required for use. They are also singularly free from serious pests and diseases.

SHALLOTS

PREPARATION OF THE GROUND.   Shallots should be grown on the same section of the ground that has been prepared for onions, i.e., ground that has been deeply dug and manured during the winter. Take the first opportunity when the ground is dry after the middle of February to break the clods and rake the surface over in order to get a tilth. If necessary, the surface should be consolidated by lightly treading.

PLANTING.   Choose a fine day towards the end of February and plant the sets 6 inches apart in a row. If two rows are grown they should be 1 foot apart. A shallow drill may be taken out, or if the soil is suitable, the sets may be pressed in until the tip of the set is just showing above the surface.

CULTIVATION.   Keep the surface clean by hoeing.

HARVESTING AND SORTING.   Towards the end of July lift the bunches of bulbs and either leave them on the surface to dry, or, if the ground is heavy and moist, lay them along a path for a few days. Tie into bundles and hang or spread them out thinly in a dry, frost-proof airy shed. Look them over at intervals to throw out any decaying bulbs. Select and put aside a sufficient number of the small bulbs (about $\frac{3}{4}$ inch in diameter) for planting in the following year.

LEEKS

1 Lifting plants from seed-bed with fork.
2 Planting 9 inches apart, in drills 15 inches apart, with trowel.
3 Plants dropped into holes 6 inches deep made with dibber.
4 Lifting crop for immediate use.

[55]

globe artichokes

GLOBE ARTICHOKES

TRUSTWORTHY CULTIVAR. Vert de Laon (obtainable as plants only).

PREPARATION OF THE GROUND. Select an open site which is well drained and away from trees or hedges. Apply a good dressing of well-rotted farmyard manure or garden compost when the soil is dug. A general fertilizer should be applied at 3 oz. per square yard before planting.

PLANTING. Rooted offsets known as 'suckers' can either be removed from the parent plant or purchased. These are planted in April in rows 2½ feet apart with 2 feet between the plants in the row. Firm planting is important.

CULTIVATION. Water should be given during dry periods. During the early part of the year the bed should be kept clean by hoeing but a mulch of well-rotted manure or compost can be applied later before the soil gets too dry. Remove old flower stems and decaying leaves in the autumn. Beds should be renewed after three successive years of cropping.

HARVESTING. The large terminal bud should be harvested first followed by the smaller heads which develop on the lateral shoots. The buds should be cut before any purple colouration of the bud scales is visible.

DISEASES. Rotting of the heads due to the petal blight fungus can be troublesome on globe artichokes. Spray with zineb soon after the buds begin to develop and repeat at fortnightly intervals until about 3 weeks before harvesting commences.

1 Taking rooted offsets (suckers) from parent plant.
2 Planting offsets in April.
3 Cutting the first terminal buds.
4 Removing decayed stems and foliage in autumn.

1

2

RUNNER BEANS

TRUSTWORTHY CULTIVARS. Staked: Achievement, Prizewinner, Streamline. Without stakes: Kelvedon Wonder, Hammond's Dwarf Scarlet (does not require pinching). Do not grow runner beans in late, cold districts.

PREPARATION OF THE GROUND. If you have not manured the plot (see p. 19) on which you are going to grow runner beans, take out during the winter a trench a spit deep, and work in a liberal dressing of rotted manure or compost into the lower spit, replacing the top spit. If possible, select a sheltered site to encourage plenty of insects for pollination.

SEED SOWING. From mid-May until the end of June, according to frost danger in the locality, sow a double row in drills 12 inches apart, and 2 to 3 inches deep, leaving 6 inches between each seed. Alternatively, runner beans may be grown without stakes, in which case the rows need not be more than 18 inches apart (see p. 60).

CULTIVATION. Thin the plants by removing each alternate seedling. Hoe as soon as the first pair of leaves has unfolded and stake immediately. Give a mulch of strawy manure or peat before the ground becomes dry, and if necessary water thoroughly when the flower buds are green or when the first red flowers open. Pinch out the shoots when they have reached the top of the stakes. If the beans are to be grown without stakes, pinch out the growing points as soon as the plants begin to run, and repeat as necessary.

HARVESTING. Pick regularly and before the pods become old and the seeds begin to swell. A few plants may be kept especially for seeds or for drying for winter use. Leave *all* the pods on these plants to ripen thoroughly, and, if the weather turns damp or rainy in the late summer, pull up the plants and finish the ripening process by hanging them in a dry airy place.

PESTS. If black bean aphid (blackfly) appears, spray or dust with malathion, dimethoate, formothion, nicotine, or derris.

DISEASES. Root-rot may injure runner beans, so be sure to change the site every season.

3

4

1

2

RUNNER BEANS

1 Taking out shallow trench 18 inches wide, 2 inches deep.
2 Drawing drills 12 inches apart, 3 inches deep.
3 Sowing seeds 6 inches apart, alternate plant to be removed later.
4 Covering the seeds.

3

4

1

2

RUNNER BEANS
1 Hoeing between plants after removal of alternate plants
   prior to staking.
2 Staking crop with hazel bean poles.
3 Wigwam supports consisting of canes for supporting
   runner beans. The plants are spaced $2\frac{1}{2}$ feet apart for
   this system.
4 Picking for use.

3

4

1

2

RUNNER BEANS DWARFED

1 Drawing drills 18 inches apart and 3 inches deep.
2 Sowing seeds 12 inches apart.
3 Covering seeds, using the feet.
4 Raking over the sown bed.

3

4

1

2

RUNNER BEANS DWARFED

1 Runner beans ready for topping.
2 First pinching of the plants to dwarf them and to save staking. [61]
3 Second pinching; pinching to be repeated weekly.
4 Picking for use.

3

4

dwarf and broad beans

DWARF BEANS

TRUSTWORTHY CULTIVARS.   Dwarf: Masterpiece and The Prince. Dwarf Stringless: Phenix Claudia, Tendergreen.

PREPARATION OF THE GROUND.   Deep digging is advisable for dwarf or French beans, and while not requiring such generous feeding as runner beans, they are best grown on ground that has received farmyard manure or compost in the autumn or winter (see p. 19).

SEED SOWING.   Make a first sowing in early May and a second one three weeks later. Break the surface down to a fine tilth a few days before sowing. Draw out drills 18 inches apart and sow the seeds 2 inches deep and $4\frac{1}{2}$ inches apart.

CULTIVATION.   Hoe regularly and water if necessary; give a little fertilizer if the land is in poor heart. Thin out to 9 inches apart. Place a few twigs among the plants to support them when they are in full bearing, as heavy rains often beat them down.

HARVESTING.   Pick the beans regularly while they are young and tender to encourage late pod formation. If any are required for winter use, leave a certain number of plants expressly for this purpose and do not pick any of the pods green. Leave them until they are quite ripe; lift them and finish their ripening under cover if bad weather sets in at the end of the summer.

BROAD BEANS

TRUSTWORTHY CULTIVARS.   The Sutton (Dwarf), Windsor, Unrivalled (Green-seeded), Imperial White Longpod, Colossal. November-sown: Aquadulce, Seville Longpod.

PREPARATION OF THE GROUND.   Select the land that has been manured in the winter, though almost any well-dug piece of land in good heart is suitable for broad beans. Break the soil down and rake it fine just before sowing.

SEED SOWING.   Sow as soon as the soil is in a fit condition in February or early March. Successional sowings may be made in late March or early April if required. Take out drills 18 inches apart and sow the seeds 9 inches apart and 3 inches deep. If sown in double rows, leave 9 inches between the rows and 2 feet between each pair of rows. The seeds should be examined for round holes, which are the exit holes of bean beetles, and all punctured seeds should be rejected.

CULTIVATION.   Hoeing must be attended to, and when the plants are in full flower pinch out the growing tuft of leaves to discourage blackfly. Make repeated pickings of the beans while they are fairly young.

PESTS.   The most serious pest which attacks broad beans is the bean aphid (blackfly); they cluster in swarms on the stems, leaf-stalks, leaves, flowers and pods in late spring and summer. Pinching out the infested tips checks the pest somewhat and permits the better development of the pods. A more effective method is to spray or dust the attacked plants with malathion, dimethoate, formothion, nicotine or derris at the very first appearance of the pest.

1

2

DWARF BEANS

1   Sowing seeds 4½ inches apart, 2 inches deep, in drills 18 inches apart.
2   Removing alternate plants.
3   Dutch hoeing between rows after thinning.
4   Picking for use.

[63]

4

3

1

2

BROAD BEANS

1 Sowing beans in double drills 24 inches apart, the drills themselves 9 inches apart and 3 inches deep.
2 Staking.
3 Pinching out the tops when plant is in flower.
4 Picking for use.

3

4

PEAS

TRUSTWORTHY CULTIVARS.   Early: Feltham First ($1\frac{1}{2}$ feet), Kelvedon Wonder ($1\frac{1}{2}$ to $1\frac{3}{4}$ feet). Early Maincrop: Early Onward (2 feet). Maincrop: Achievement (4 to 5 feet), Onward ($2\frac{1}{2}$ feet). Height is approximate and can vary from year to year.

PREPARATION OF THE GROUND.   The ground should be well manured in the autumn or winter as recommended on p. 19, since peas appreciate generous treatment and on well cultivated land withstand drought better.

SEED SOWING.   Begin sowing towards the end of February or early March when the soil conditions are suitable. Follow at intervals of about three weeks, according to require-ments, until June. Draw out flat drills (see p. 66) 6 to 8 inches broad and 2 to 3 inches deep. Sow in three rows in the drills 3 inches apart each way, about 20 seeds to the foot. Another method is to draw narrow V-shaped drills (see p. 66) 2 to 3 inches deep, and sow the seeds in one single row at the bottom of the drill. Sow a few extra at the end of the row to supply plants for filling up gaps. The rows should be spaced according to the height of the cultivar being sown, e.g. the variety Onward should be sown in rows $2\frac{1}{2}$ feet apart. Where space is limited it is better to dispense with the tall varieties and make repeated sowings at intervals of three weeks of the same early dwarf variety.

CULTIVATION.   As soon as the peas are 2 inches high, hoe carefully between the rows to aerate the soil and keep down weeds. Stake the tall varieties, using either pea boughs or netting, as soon as two pairs of leaves have opened. In dry weather water when the first flowers appear and again at podlet stage. A mulch of peat or strawy manure between the rows will help to conserve the moisture in the soil.

HARVESTING.   Pick the pods regularly as they become ready. Peas required for drying for winter use should be gathered from plants reserved for the purpose and all the pods left on these plants to ripen thoroughly. Should the weather turn damp or rainy as these peas near the end of their ripening pull the entire plants and hang them in bundles in a dry, airy place to finish ripening.

DISEASES AND PESTS.   Foot-rot may injure peas, so be sure to cultivate the ground well to avoid heavy, wet soil conditions, especially with early peas, and be sure to change the site every season. Mildew can injure the later ones, especially if removal of the finished, early rows, which soon become mildewed is neglected. In some seasons spraying with dinocap to check mildew may be necessary. Thrips and pea moth are controlled by spraying with BHC 10 days after the first flowers appear and greenfly may be checked by one of the insecticides recommended for blackfly on beans (p. 62).

1

2

PEAS

1 Drawing flat bottom drill 2 to 3 inches deep.
2 Sowing seeds in 3 rows 2 to 3 inches apart.
3 Drawing V-shaped drill 2 to 3 inches deep.
4 Sowing seeds in 1 single row in V-shaped drill.

3

4

1

2

PEAS

1   Staking, keeping sticks upright; leaving space for plant
     development.
2   Sticks topped and toppings used to fill in base.
3   Wire netting supporting young plants.
4   Wire netting supporting crop approaching maturity.

[67]

3

4

brassicas, cabbages

BRASSICAS

BRUSSELS SPROUTS, cabbages, cauliflowers (summer and winter), kales, savoys and sprouting broccoli are all raised on a seed-bed and transplanted later. A great economy in seeds may be effected if several gardeners will combine together and arrange for one of them to raise the required plants, or plants may be bought.

CABBAGES

TRUSTWORTHY CULTIVARS. Spring maturing—small head: April, Wheeler's Imperial. Medium head: Early Durham, Myatt's Early Offenham. Summer maturing—small round head: Fillgap. Small to medium pointed head: Greyhound. Small to medium round head: Early Golden Acre. Medium to large round head: Golden Acre, Primo. Autumn and winter maturing—drumhead: Christmas Drumhead, January King, Winter White. Pointed: Winningstadt.

SPRING-SOWN CABBAGES FOR SUMMER USE

PREPARATION OF THE GROUND. For summer cabbages, if the ground is in poor heart, dig in a little manure. Dig the ground as it becomes vacant and leave it rough until planting time; then break it down and firm it.

SEED SOWING. Sow on prepared seed-beds (see p. 25) about $\frac{3}{4}$ inch deep during early April.

TRANSPLANTING. Should the ground be dry, soak the seed-bed with water the night before lifting for transplanting. Set the plants out $1\frac{1}{2}$ feet apart each way during early June.

CULTIVATION. Hoe frequently during the summer.

SUMMER-SOWN CABBAGES FOR AUTUMN AND WINTER USE

SEED SOWING. Sow the seeds $\frac{3}{4}$ inch deep during May on prepared seed-beds.

TRANSPLANTING. Set out the plants during July on ground manured for the previous crop. Plant in rows 2 feet apart with $1\frac{1}{2}$ feet between the plants in the row.

CULTIVATION. Hoe frequently during late summer and autumn.

EARLY AUTUMN-SOWN CABBAGES FOR SPRING USE

PREPARATION OF THE GROUND. Plant in soil which received manure for the previous crop. This crop will benefit from deep cultivation.

SEED SOWING.   Sow in rows 6 inches apart on a prepared bed (see p. 25) at the end of July in the north and during the first two weeks of August in the south.

TRANSPLANTING.   Transplant from the seed-bed in mid-September to mid-October, allowing 18 inches between the rows and 9 inches between the plants, if every other plant is to be used later for spring greens before the cabbages mature. If hearted cabbages are required plant 18 inches apart each way.

CULTIVATION. Hoe when the ground is in a suitable condition. Before the plants begin to touch each other, cut out every other plant for use as spring greens. Early in March hoe in a dressing of 2 oz. of nitrate of soda or sulphate of ammonia per square yard.

PESTS AND DISEASES.   Flea beetles or turnip fly attack the seed-leaves of Brassicas. Dust or spray the seedlings with BHC applied as soon as the leaves appear above ground, and repeat at weekly intervals until the rough leaf stage is reached. This pest is only serious in dry weather and can be checked by watering every evening after sunset until the plants are growing freely.

Cabbage caterpillars comprise those of the large and small white butterflies and the moth, all of which feed on leaf tissues causing extensive damage. The late summer attack is the most serious. Crush the egg clusters of the large butterfly, and hand-pick the colonies of caterpillars. Dust the plants with BHC or derris, or, if within 2 weeks of picking, spray with derris or trichlorphon.

Cabbage root fly chiefly affects cabbages and cauliflowers soon after planting out, the legless white maggots eating the roots and tunnelling in the stems. Dig up and burn attacked plants, together with the soil immediately around the roots. Dust round transplants with 4% calomel dust or drench the roots with lindane 4 days after planting out. Lindane will not be effective in areas where cabbage root fly is resistant to organochlorine insecticides. Trichlorphon, applied as a spray-strength solution watered into the soil around transplants on two or three occasions in the month following planting out, may give adequate protection.

Cabbage aphids and cabbage whitefly should be eradicated with malathion, dimethoate, formothion, or nicotine plus a wetting agent as soon as they are seen, otherwise they get under the heart leaves where they are difficult to reach.

Birds, in particular pigeons, may cause severe damage to the foliage. It is very difficult to prevent this damage but temporary netting may be used to protect young plants and various scaring devices may have some effect.

The most troublesome disease is club root or finger and toe. The remedy in severe cases is to lime the ground with a dressing of 28 lb. per square rod of ground chalk or limestone. If hydrated lime is used about 20 lb. per square rod will be sufficient. In succeeding years a light dressing—14 lb. per square rod—should be given. Make every effort to secure the proper drainage of the ground by thorough cultivation and deep digging. As a further precaution the seedlings can be treated before planting by dipping their roots in a paste made of 4% calomel dust mixed into a thick cream with water and a little clay or flour. The same fungicide can also be applied to the seedbed at $1\frac{1}{2}$ oz. per square yard or 1 oz. per 5-foot run of drill.

1

2

GREEN CROPS, CABBAGES, ETC.

1 Watering seed-bed prior to lifting plants for planting out.
2 Lifting plants with a fork.
3 Firming the plant with dibber.

3

GREEN CROPS, CABBAGES, ETC.

1 Lifting plants with trowel, preserving roots in ball of earth.
2 Firming the plants by inserting blade of trowel about 2 inches from the plant and pressing towards it.
3 Firming the plant with the handle of the trowel.
4 Testing the plant for firmness of planting. Note torn leaf in the hand.

[71]

1

PLANTING CABBAGES

1 Firming the ground by treading.
2 Drawing drills about 18 to 24 inches apart, 2 inches deep.
3 Planting.
4 Watering after planting.

2

3

4

SAVOYS

TRUSTWORTHY CULTIVARS. Early: Best of all. Late: Omega, Ormskirk Late, Rear-guard.

PREPARATION OF THE GROUND. Savoys should be grown on land that has been manured for the previous crop. Hoe in a dressing of 2 oz. of superphosphate and 1 oz. of sulphate of potash per square yard before transplanting.

SEED SOWING. Sow $\frac{3}{4}$ inch deep during May on a prepared seed-bed (see p. 25).

TRANSPLANTING. In July or early August set out the plants 2 feet by $1\frac{1}{2}$ feet apart on firm ground that has been cleared of previous crops (see p. 101).

CULTIVATION. Hoe periodically during the summer. Remove decaying leaves during late autumn and winter.

KALES

TRUSTWORTHY CULTIVARS. Cottager's, Dwarf Curled, Hungry Gap (see p. 120).

PREPARATION OF THE GROUND. See savoys above.

SEED SOWING. Sow the seeds $\frac{3}{4}$ inch deep from the end of April and during May on a prepared seed-bed (see p. 25). The cultivar Hungry Gap should be sown where it is to crop on ground that has been cleared of peas or early potatoes. Sow thinly during the first half of July in rows 18 inches apart and thin by stages to 18 inches apart. It is a valuable crop in cold districts for use in April or May.

TRANSPLANTING. Set the plants out 2 feet apart each way during July or early August.

CULTIVATION. Plant firmly and hoe regularly.

BRUSSELS SPROUTS

TRUSTWORTHY CULTIVARS. F_1 hybrids: Indra, Peer Gynt, Thor. Open pollinated: Ashwell, Market Rearguard, Irish Elegance.

PREPARATION OF THE GROUND. Brussels sprouts should be grown on firm ground in good heart, supplemented by a dressing of 5 lb. of superphosphate mixed with 2 lb. of sulphate of potash per square rod.

SEED SOWING. Sow on prepared seed-beds (see p. 25) from mid-March to mid-April.

TRANSPLANTING. Plants should be transplanted, not more than $2\frac{1}{2}$ feet apart each way, in late May or June. Water the seed-beds the night before lifting for transplanting.

CULTIVATION. Plant firmly. Hoe regularly and draw a little soil to the stems about a month after planting. Remove the lower leaves from the plants as they begin to turn yellow in the autumn, but not before (see p. 76).

HARVESTING. Gather the sprouts as they become ready, beginning from the bottom of the stem (see p. 74).

PESTS. See cabbage.

1

2

3

BRUSSELS
SPROUTS

1 Well-developed plant,
    showing tight
    'buttons'.

2 Badly-developed plant,
    showing loose
    'buttons'.

3 Correct method of
    gathering, com-
    mencing at base of
    plant.

CAULIFLOWERS

TRUSTWORTHY CULTIVARS. Summer maturing: All the Year Round, Classic, Snowball. Autumn maturing: Boomerang, Kangaroo, South Pacific.

PREPARATION OF THE GROUND. Cauliflowers require land in good heart. Dig deeply and manure well. Hoe in 1 to 2 oz. of superphosphate per square yard before transplanting.

SEED SOWING. Seeds of the summer cultivars can be sown under glass in January or on prepared seed-beds (see p. 25) about ¾ inch deep during March and April. Autumn heading cultivars should be sown at the end of April until mid-May on prepared seed-beds in the open ground.

TRANSPLANTING. The summer cultivars can be transplanted from March to June, setting the plants out from 18 inches to 2 feet apart each way. Autumn cultivars are transplanted 2 to 2½ feet each way during late June and July.

CULTIVATION. Hoe regularly. When the curds have formed protect them from the light and weather by breaking a leaf or two over them if not required for immediate use (see p. 76). If growth is slow dress with 1 oz. of nitrate of soda or sulphate of ammonia per square yard.

PESTS. See cabbage.

BROCCOLI (WINTER CAULIFLOWER)

TRUSTWORTHY CULTIVARS. Superb Early White (January–February), St. George (April), Late Queen (May). Winter cauliflower is liable to be killed by severe frost; sprouting broccoli, Late Purple Sprouting, is hardy and in unfavourable districts the choice may be restricted to this variety. The Roscoff cultivars should only be grown in mild districts.

SEED SOWING. Sow the seeds on a prepared seed-bed ¾ inch deep (see p. 25) from mid-April until mid-May, according to the variety.

PREPARATION OF THE GROUND. Broccoli should be grown on firm ground which has not been disturbed since the previous crop has been cleared. Dress with a mixture of 2 oz. of superphosphate and 1 oz. of sulphate of potash per square yard, hoed in before transplanting.

TRANSPLANTING. Transplant 2 feet apart each way during June and July as the ground becomes available.

CULTIVATION. Hoe as required. Broccoli must be grown hard to stand the winter.

1

2

BRUSSELS SPROUTS AND CAULIFLOWERS

1 Drawing up soil round stems for support.
2 Breaking off the lower yellow leaves in autumn.
3 Breaking leaf for protection over curd of cauliflower.
4 Heeling over winter cauliflower for winter protection.

3

4

SPINACH

TRUSTWORTHY CULTIVARS.   Seed round: Dominant, Greenmarket. Seed prickly: Giant-Leaved Prickly.

PREPARATION OF THE GROUND.   Spinach should be grown on well-manured ground (see Plan, p. 15).

SEED SOWINGS.   Summer crop: Make successional sowings from February to May of the summer varieties in drills 1 inch deep and 12 to 15 inches apart.

Winter crop: Sow in August in drills 1 inch deep and 12 inches apart, and make another sowing in September.

CULTIVATION.   Thin the plants as soon as they are large enough to handle. Thin in the first place to 3 inches apart. Remove alternate plants after about a fortnight and use them. Hoe regularly and water during dry weather.

DISEASES.   Downy mildew, which causes yellow blotches on the upper leaf surfaces and a greyish mould on the lower surfaces, can be troublesome especially if the plants are crowded or drainage is poor. Proper thinning of plants and good drainage will help to prevent this disease, which is difficult to control, although spraying with zineb or a copper fungicide may check it.

SPINACH BEET

THIS VEGETABLE IS also known as perpetual spinach as it provides a supply of leaves over a long period during autumn and winter.

PREPARATION OF THE GROUND.   See spinach above.

SEED SOWING.   Sow in drills 1 inch deep and 18 inches apart during April and July.

CULTIVATION.   See spinach above.

Gather the leaves when they reach a usable size; coarse leaves not required for use should be picked to encourage young growth.

1   Picking summer spinach.
2   Crop of summer spinach ready for use.

CELERY

TRUSTWORTHY CULTIVARS. New Dwarf White, Solid White.

PREPARATION OF THE GROUND. Ground for celery should be richly prepared. Take out trenches 15 inches wide and 1 foot deep. Work manure or compost into the bottom of the trench. Return soil to the trench to within 3 inches of the level of the ground.

SEED SOWING. If greenhouse heat is available, sow the seeds in pots during March. Prick off the seedlings into boxes and harden them off in cold frames. Alternatively, buy a box of plants from your local nurseryman.

TRANSPLANTING. Set the plants out carefully in late May or June in double rows 1 foot apart and 10 inches between the plants. Water them in.

CULTIVATION. Water copiously to encourage steady growth if the weather is dry; dust with weathered soot at intervals of about ten days. Before earthing, tie the stems loosely just below the leaves and remove any suckers that may have appeared. Begin earthing as soon as the plants are about 12 to 15 inches high. Always see that the ground is thoroughly moist before beginning to earth up. Make the first earthing very slight; the second and third, at intervals of about three weeks, may be more generous. Be careful not to let any soil fall into the heart of the plant and never earth higher than the base of the leaves. The final earthing should cover all the stems, right up to the leaves, and the soil should be sloped away neatly. During late winter, place some bracken or other protective material over the plants to carry the crop on as late as possible.

PESTS AND DISEASES. The chief pest is the celery fly or leaf-miner. Brown blisters appear on the leaves from May onwards. Watch seedling plants carefully for blistered leaves, which should be removed and destroyed or crushed between the fingers. Apply nitrate of soda (a heaped teaspoonful per square yard) to stimulate growth. Spray with malathion, dimethoate or trichlorphon if necessary. For the control of slugs and snails see p. 28.

Leaf spot shows as brown patches on leaves and stems. This disease may be carried with the seed. Be sure to buy clean reliable seed and spray with Bordeaux mixture or zineb as soon as the trouble appears, repeating this if necessary.

SELF-BLANCHING CELERY

TRUSTWORTHY CULTIVARS. Golden Self Blanching, Lathom Blanching. Green Self-Blanching: Greensleeves.

PREPARATION OF THE GROUND. Incorporate plenty of farmyard manure or garden compost when digging the ground in preparation for this crop.

SEED SOWING. Sow the seeds in pots not earlier than the third week of March. Prick off the seedlings into boxes and gradually harden them off in cold frames.

TRANSPLANTING. No trenches are required as the plants are transplanted on level ground. Set the plants out 9 inches apart each way in late May or June, using a trowel for transplanting. It is best to plant in blocks rather than single rows.

1

2

CELERY

1 Trench one spit deep, 15 inches wide.
2 Trench cleaned of 'crumbs'.
3 Manure placed on bottom of trench.
4 Digging in manure.

3

4

CULTIVATION. The plants should be given generous quantities of water weekly unless the weather is exceptionally wet. No earthing is necessary, but all suckers should be removed as they appear. Where the crop is not grown in frames, a little straw should be tucked between the plants growing on the outside of the block to assist blanching. The crop is less hardy than celery grown in trenches and will be damaged by a number of sharp frosts.

PESTS AND DISEASES. See celery.

1

2

CELERY

1 Plants ready for planting out.
2 Planting double line 12 inches between rows and 10 inches between plants.
3 Watering after planting.
4 Tying plants prior to first earthing.

3

4

5

6

CELERY

5 First earthing.
6 Final earthing.

SELF-BLANCHING CELERY

1 Planting self-blanching celery 9 inches apart each way
   in cold frames.
2 Crop of self-blanching celery ready for use.

1

2

1

3

2

4

CELERIAC

1 Drawing drills 18 inches apart and 2 inches deep.
2 Planting out 12 inches apart.
3 Removing a few of the older lower leaves.
4 Lifting the crop with a fork for immediate use or storing.

CELERIAC (TURNIP-ROOTED CELERY)

TRUSTWORTHY CULTIVAR. Globus.

PREPARATION OF THE GROUND. Celeriac repays good cultivation. Choose, if possible, ground that has received a dressing of farmyard manure.

SEED SOWING. Plants may be raised as advised for celery, or they may be purchased.

CULTIVATION. Plant out the seedling plants in shallow drills 18 inches apart, leaving 12 inches between the plants. Firm planting is necessary. Give copious supplies of water during the summer months and remove side shoots as soon as they appear. It is also a good practice periodically to remove a few of the older leaves (see p. 82). Hoe regularly.

HARVESTING AND STORING. The roots may be used direct from the ground or lifted in November and stored in the same way as carrots in a shed where they can be protected from frost.

PESTS AND DISEASES. See celery (p. 78).

LETTUCES

TRUSTWORTHY CULTIVARS. For continuous cloches: Unrivalled. For continuous cold frames and Dutch lights: Delta, Early French Frame, Kloek, Knap, May King. For summer use in the open: Cobham Green, Mildura, Avondefiance, Great Lakes (curly crisp), Webb's Wonderful (curly crisp), Little Gem (Cos) and Lobjoits Green Cos (Cos). For early spring use, grown without protection during the winter: Imperial, Winter Crop and Winter Density (Cos).

PREPARATION OF THE GROUND. Lettuces are best grown on the piece of ground you have manured during the autumn or winter. Dig the ground thoroughly and leave it rough until planting time. Then break down the lumps and rake the surface to a fine tilth.

CONTINUOUS CLOCHES. Make the first sowing under continuous cloches about October 10th to 20th in shallow drills 6 inches apart. Transplant the seedlings under further cloches from the middle of December onwards in rows 12 inches apart with 12 inches between the plants. Further sowings can be made between the middle of January and the end of February and the seedlings transplanted under other cloches for later crops.

CONTINUOUS COLD FRAMES AND DUTCH LIGHTS. For cutting in early spring sow in shallow drills 6 inches apart from October 10th to 20th. Transplant the seedlings in cold frames or under Dutch lights from the middle of December onwards, spacing the plants $8\frac{1}{2}$ inches each way. For later crops sow from the middle of January until the end of February and transplant the seedlings $8\frac{1}{2}$ inches apart each way in frames or under Dutch lights. For an autumn or early winter crop sow the cultivar May King in the open ground not later than the first week of August. Transplant the seedlings in frames $8\frac{1}{2}$ inches apart each way, and cover the plants with glass about the middle of September.

SUMMER USE IN THE OPEN. Sow in $\frac{1}{2}$ inch deep drills in the open ground, half a row at a time, in rows 1 foot apart. Make the first sowing in early March and continue at fortnightly intervals until July. Thin the seedlings when the first pairs of true leaves have well formed. The final distance apart in the rows should be from 9 to 12 inches (see p. 86).

EARLY SPRING USE, GROWN WITHOUT PROTECTION DURING THE WINTER. Sow during the end of August or early September in drills 1 foot apart and $\frac{1}{2}$ inch deep. The seedlings should be thinned lightly in early October, or a second row can be planted using the thinnings and transplanting 3 inches apart. Commencing in early spring, the plants should be thinned from time to time to a final distance of 9 to 12 inches apart (see p. 86).

PESTS AND DISEASES. At the first signs of greenfly spray or dust immediately with malathion or nicotine. If nearly ready for cutting use a derris spray instead. For the control of slugs and snails see p. 28.

The important disease of lettuces is the one known as grey mould in which the stem is attacked at soil-level by a fungus and the plant quickly wilts. It is important to provide the best soil conditions to encourage good rooting and to plant out carefully. Quintozene raked into the soil before sowing or transplanting will help to prevent this disease and overwintering plants can be sprayed every 3–4 weeks with thiram.

ENDIVE

TRUSTWORTHY CULTIVARS. For summer use: Green Curled; for late autumn and winter use: Batavian Broad Leaved.

PREPARATION OF THE GROUND. As for lettuces.

SEED SOWING. For an early crop sow the seeds in drills 1 foot apart during June. Make the main sowing in July at the same distance apart. The Batavian type may be sown in drills 15 inches apart in August and early September to provide winter salad material.

CULTIVATION. Thin the plants in two stages, leaving the curled varieties 1 foot apart and the Batavian varieties 15 inches apart. Keep the ground clean by hoeing regularly and blanch the plants a short time before they are required for use by covering the plant with a pot or even a slate or a piece of wood. Continuous cloches, Dutch lights or continuous cold frames can also be used for blanching provided some shading or covering is applied to the glass to exclude light. Plants for winter supplies should be lifted before danger of severe frost and placed under darkened cloches or Dutch lights or in boxes of soil in a shed or cellar from which the light is excluded to blanch them.

1

2

3

4

LETTUCES

1 Planting 2 rows 1 foot apart under continuous cloches, spacing the plants 1 foot apart.
2 Planting under continuous cloches completed and ends covered.
3 Planting under Dutch lights, spacing the plants 8½ inches apart each way.
4 Planting under continuous cold frames, spacing the plants 8½ inches apart each way.
5 Crop approaching maturity under Dutch lights.

5

1

2

[86]

LETTUCES

1 Plants ready for first thinning.
2 First thinning: plants 3 inches apart.
3 Second thinning: plants 6 inches apart.
4 Plants ready for use: 12 inches apart.

3

4

RADISHES

TRUSTWORTHY CULTIVARS.   Round: Cherry Belle, Saxa, Scarlet Globe and Sparkler. Cylindrical: French Breakfast.

PREPARATION OF THE GROUND.   Any well-cultivated ground in good heart that has been brought to a good tilth is suitable for radishes.

SEED SOWING IN THE OPEN.   Make successional sowings very thinly as required from early March until May at intervals of about a fortnight or three weeks. Autumn sowings can be made if desired, but if sown in the summer radishes bolt immediately and are hot and dry.

CONTINUOUS CLOCHES, DUTCH LIGHTS AND CONTINUOUS COLD FRAMES.   Sow very thinly, either broadcast or in shallow drills spaced 6 inches apart from January to early March. Little thinning will be required if seed is sown thinly.

I

RADISHES
1 Sowing radishes in shallow drills 6 inches apart under continuous cold frames.
2 Pulling crop of radishes from under continuous cold frame.

2

tomatoes, herbs

TOMATOES

TRUSTWORTHY CULTIVARS.   Ailsa Craig, Harbinger, Leader, Moneymaker, Amateur (bush).

PREPARATION OF THE GROUND.   Choose a warm, sheltered spot if possible—preferably a border beside a fence or wall. Dig thoroughly and apply a general fertilizer at the rate of 3 oz. per square yard 10 to 14 days before planting out.

SEED SOWING.   Sow seeds in boxes in a greenhouse in late March or early April. Prick off into pots and harden off in a cold frame. Keep the young plants sturdy and prevent them from becoming drawn. Alternatively, purchase a box of plants from your local nurseryman.

CULTIVATION.   Plant out after all danger of frost is over—usually from early June onwards. Allow 18 inches between the plants, and if more than one row is grown allow 2½ feet between the rows. Place a good, strong stake to each plant at planting time (see p. 89). Pinch out the side shoots regularly and tie the main shoot to the stake as required. When four or five trusses have set, pinch out the top growth. The bush cultivars are not staked and the side shoots and main shoots are allowed to develop without pinching out. The plants should be given a mulch of straw or other similar material to prevent the lower fruits becoming soiled. In September the plants will still have many green fruits. Cut the ties and draw the stakes; lay the plants along the ground, keeping the fruits off the soil by means of short forked sticks. Then cover with continuous cloches and the fruits will ripen.

HARVESTING AND STORING.   The season of tomatoes may be prolonged by picking the late fruits when they are just beginning to turn colour and storing them, wrapped in soft paper, in a drawer or cupboard in a temperature of 45°–50°. They will then ripen slowly and keep up a supply of fruits until the end of the year.

DISEASES.   Blight must be guarded against by spraying with a liquid copper spray, zineb or maneb as soon as most of the plants have been stopped (i.e. the tops pinched out). In cool wet seasons repeat at 2 to 3 week intervals.

HERBS

HERBS are of especial value in the vegetable garden as they add flavour to many dishes. They may be grown as an edging alongside a plot or bed or on a small separate bed where room is available. Mint will require a small bed and can be increased by cuttings or division of the roots in March.

Make a sowing of parsley in March and a second sowing in July for succession, spacing the rows 12 inches apart. Thin to 6 inches apart. Chives are very valuable as flavouring in soups and salads in place of onions. They can be raised from seeds or division. Cut the growth down at intervals for use and thus encourage fresh growth. Sage and thyme can be raised from seeds and should be sown in shallow drills in April and thinned or transplanted to 6 inches apart for thyme and 1 foot apart for sage. Sage and thyme can also be increased by division in March.

DRYING FOR WINTER USE.   Mint, sage and thyme may be dried for winter use. Gather and make into a bunch to be hung in a dry, airy place. When dry, spread them on a newspaper before a fire and rub them into a powder which should then be stored in a corked bottle until wanted.

1

2

TOMATOES

1 Tying plants after completion of staking and planting.
2 Showing side growth to be removed.
3 Stopping after formation of 4 trusses.
4 First picking for use.

[89]

3

4

cucumbers, marrows

RIDGE CUCUMBERS

TRUSTWORTHY CULTIVARS. Baton Vert, Bedfordshire Prize Ridge, Burpee Hybrid.

PREPARATION OF THE GROUND. Prepare a low mound of rich material and cover with 2 to 3 inches of fine soil, or prepare well-manured ground by raking the surface level.

SEED SOWING. Sow seeds in groups 2 to $2\frac{1}{2}$ feet apart and about 1 inch deep at the end of May or early in June, thinning later to leave the strongest plant at each station. The rows should be spaced 3 feet apart.

CULTIVATION. Water freely during dry weather. It is not necessary to pinch out the top of the plants.

HARVESTING. Cut the fruits while young to encourage continued production.

VEGETABLE MARROWS

TRUSTWORTHY CULTIVARS. Bush: Bush Green, Early Gem (F_1 hybrid), Tender and True. Trailing: Long Green Trailing, Table Dainty. Courgettes are baby marrows cut when 4 inches long and cooked whole. Suitable cultivar: Courgette (F_1 hybrid).

PREPARATION OF THE GROUND. In a sunny corner of the plot or garden, dig in some well-rotted manure or compost (see p. 91).

   Marrows are sometimes grown on a heap of rich soil, such as compost or turf that has been stacked.

SEED SOWING. Sow in the open towards the end of May. Place four or five seeds in groups about 6 inches apart and 1 inch deep, and finally thin to two plants 12 to 15 inches apart (see p. 91).

CULTIVATION. Hoe regularly and water copiously in dry weather. Special care must be taken to ensure that marrows do not suffer from want of water.

HARVESTING AND STORING. For summer use, cut marrows when they are 6–8 inches long, otherwise the plants will not bear fruits freely. Leave a number of fruits to grow to their full size and ripen thoroughly for storing. Before danger of frost threatens, cut these late marrows and hang them in a dry, airy, frost-proof place.

DISEASES. Marrows are very susceptible to infection by cucumber mosaic virus which causes stunting of plants, puckering and mottling of leaves, and mottling and distortion of fruits which are reduced in size. There is no chemical control and diseased plants should be removed and burned as soon as the first symptoms are seen.

1

2

VEGETABLE MARROWS

1   Placing manure in bottom of bed taken out one spit deep.
2   Sowing 4 or 5 seeds 6 inches apart, 1 inch deep.
3   Thinning, retaining two plants.
4   Ready for use (variety: Green Bush).

3

4

ASPARAGUS

TRUSTWORTHY CULTIVARS. From seed: Martha Washington, Connover's Colossal, Argenteiul. From plants: Connover's Colossal, Kidner's Pedigree, Superior (F_1 hybrid).

PREPARATION OF THE GROUND. Asparagus will grow on most soils but good drainage and freedom from perennial weeds are essential. Apply manure or garden compost during the autumn or early winter preceding planting. Fork over the ground in February to promote a tilth for planting.

SEED SOWING. Sow in good soil during March or early April, in rows $1\frac{1}{2}$ feet apart. Single seedlings to 6 inches apart. Plants raised in this way can be planted on a permanent site in March or April of the following year.

PLANTING. Under present conditions best results are normally obtained with one year old plants. Plant in March or April in single rows spaced $4\frac{1}{2}$ feet apart with $1\frac{1}{2}$ feet between the plants in the row. Prepare trench 12 inches wide and 8 inches deep; replace mound of soil 3 inches deep in bottom of trench (see p. 93). Plant asparagus and cover roots with 2 to 3 inches of fine soil and gradually fill trench by drawing a little soil on to the plants each time the soil is hoed during the first season. A general fertilizer should be applied at 3 oz. per square yard in late February or early March each year.

CUTTING. Do not cut any shoots for the first two years after planting. In the third year after planting cut for 6 weeks and in the following years for 8 weeks. Cut all sizes of shoots at each cutting. After cutting has ceased the green foliage should not be cut for decorative purposes.

LATER CULTIVATION. Cut down the plants when the foliage changes colour in the autumn before many ripe berries from the asparagus drop to the soil. Mound up soil several inches deep over the row; this can be done in the autumn if the soil is heavy otherwise the operation can be deferred until March.

PESTS. Asparagus beetle adults and larvae eat foliage which may be completely stripped. When damage is noticed spray with BHC or derris. Use only derris in the cutting season.

1

2

ASPARAGUS

1 Asparagus trench prepared for planting. Note mound in bottom of trench.

2 Covering roots of newly planted asparagus with soil.

3 Cutting.

4 Cutting down plants in autumn.

[93]

3

4

seakale beet, artichokes, rhubarb

SEAKALE BEET

SEAKALE BEET IS useful to provide a change from the ordinary run of green vegetables. It is sometimes known as silver beet or swiss chard. The leaves are first stripped from the stalks and the mid-ribs and cooked in the same way as spinach; the stalks and the mid-ribs can then be cooked separately in the same way as seakale.

PREPARATION OF THE GROUND. Seakale beet should be grown on ground in good heart. It appreciates good soil.

SEED SOWING. Seeds should be sown in drills 1 inch deep and 18 inches apart during April.

CULTIVATION. Begin to thin the plants as soon as they are large enough to handle. The first thinning may be given leaving the plants at 4 inches apart. After about a fortnight the alternate plants may be taken out. Attend to hoeing during the summer and water during dry weather.

JERUSALEM ARTICHOKES

THESE USEFUL PLANTS can be grown in any odd corner of the garden and will put up with rougher conditions than is appropriate to other vegetables, although they will repay good cultivation.

They are very useful as a summer screen for a shed, manure or compost heap.

Plant in February or March in drills 4 to 6 inches deep and 2 feet 6 inches apart, allowing 15 inches between each tuber.

Hoe frequently on all favourable occasions. Cut the stalks down in early winter; the tubers may be left in the ground and lifted as they are wanted for use. When the crop is lifted reserve a number of tubers for replanting to provide a supply for the following year. The replanting may follow immediately upon the operation of lifting.

RHUBARB

TRUSTWORTHY CULTIVARS. Early: Timperley Early. Second Early: Hawke's Champagne. Maincrop: The Sutton.

Rhubarb forms a valuable crop for tarts and puddings early in the year before any fruit is available, and even the smallest garden or allotment can find space for half a dozen plants.

The piece of ground selected should be deeply dug and well manured, because the plants have to stand for several years. Apply a general fertilizer at 3 oz. per square yard 10 to 14 days before planting out.

Divide established roots to leave one good bud on each set and plant either in October or March; do not pull any sticks in the first year but keep the ground clean. Even in the second year only pull lightly. Be careful to cut out flowering shoots as they appear.

In established beds one or two strong roots can be selected in December for forwarding. Obtain a grape-barrel or a box for each plant, and knock out the top and bottom. Put the barrel or box over the root and replace the lid in position. Then pack round the outside of the container with long, strawy manure or, failing that, with leaves, hay or bracken.

SWEET CORN

TRUSTWORTHY CULTIVARS.   Early (F_1 hybrids): Canada Cross (John Innes Hybrid), Earliking, Kelvedon Glory. Mid-season (F_1 hybrid): North Star.

PREPARATION OF THE GROUND.   Choose an open position away from shade and apply some garden compost or well-rotted manure when the ground is being dug. Apply a general fertilizer at 3 oz. per square yard 10 to 14 days before planting or sowing.

SEED SOWING.   Seeds can be sown under glass during April by sowing two seeds to each 3-inch pot and removing weakest plant after germination. The seedlings are transplanted in the open at the end of May in rows $2\frac{1}{2}$ feet apart with 15 inches between the plants. Alternatively, seeds are sown in the open ground about the middle of May; two seeds being placed in stations 15 inches apart in drills $\frac{3}{4}$ to 1 inch deep. The rows are spaced $2\frac{1}{2}$ feet apart. Sweet corn is always best planted or sown in a block or a number of short rows and not in one long row.

CULTIVATION.   Where the seed is sown direct into the open ground the plants should be singled to leave the strongest plant at each station. Hoeing should be shallow and a little soil pulled up to the plants will provide additional support against wind. It is not necessary to remove the suckers or side growths. Water should be given during dry weather.

HARVESTING.   Sweet corn is ready for harvesting when the silk at the end of the ear or cob has turned dark brown in colour and the cob is fully developed and tight when grasped in the hand. The crop is gathered by snapping the cobs from the main stem of the plant. Sweet corn should be used as soon as possible after harvesting.

PESTS.   The larvae of the frit fly burrow in the tissues of the growing point, stunting the growth of the main shoot and producing twisted and ragged leaves. Spray with BHC when the plant has two or three leaves. Where attacks occur regularly avoid sowing in the open during May. Instead, sow under glass in April and plant out at the end of May.

SWEET CORN
1   Sowing 2 seeds 15 inches apart, 1 inch deep, in drills
$2\frac{1}{2}$ feet apart.
2   Removing weakest plant at each station.

WEED CONTROL

Try and avoid sites infested with perennial weeds when sowing small vegetable seeds. The cultivation of a crop of early potatoes followed by a cover crop of Italian ryegrass will do much to reduce the infestation. The ryegrass should be dug into the soil when about 8 to 9 inches high. Annual weeds should be destroyed by hoeing or chemical means before they seed. Before sowing or planting vegetables, the herbicide paraquat/diquat salts can be used as a spray to control annual broadleaved weeds and tops of perennial weeds and grasses. Paraquat/diquat salts can also be used to control these weeds between widely spaced crops such as beans, Brussels sprouts, peas and rhubarb provided every precaution is taken to avoid spray drift on to foliage of vegetables. Dalapon will control couch in such crops as asparagus. Cresylic acid will kill many annual weeds and the tops of perennial weeds particularly when cleaning beds in the autumn. *When using any horticultural chemical first read the instructions and secondly follow them. No attempt should be made to store liquid of paraquat/diquat salts and on no account should liquid be transferred to bottles that do not have a "poison" label.*

WEED CONTROL

1 Spraying paraquat/diquat salts on to weeds between Brussels sprouts.
2 Weeds killed between Brussels sprouts after spraying with paraquat/diquat salts.

1

2

SUCCESSIONAL CROPPING AND INTERCROPPING

IN ORDER TO MAKE the best use of a limited piece of ground, it is necessary to plant the spaces that are empty during the early part of the season, or again, those from which crops are cleared early in the summer, with other quick-growing crops that can be cleared again before the next main crop comes to be grown in the same place. For example, lettuces are wanted nearly all the year round, but it is not necessary to set apart much ground for them, for short rows can be sown between the rows of widely spaced plants—peas, for example. Catch crop rows of carrots and beetroots can also be inter-sown to be pulled and used young during the summer, without drawing upon the main crops of which the roots are to be stored for winter use. Lettuces and radishes above all other vegetables should be sown repeatedly in short rows in order to provide a con-tinuous succession of young material to be gathered as it can be used, instead of a large crop of mature plants which will be far more than any one household can use at the time. The gardener who is growing these crops for sale wants them to come in all together, so that he gets a consignment for market; not so the gardener who is catering for his own family. Carrots should be treated in the same way, for young carrots are very valuable as food and pleasanter to eat than the main crop, which still is of the first importance when stored for winter use.

The plans on pages 16–18 list the successional and catch crops which can be grown.

Looking first at section 1, at the end of the section are runner beans and shallots as the main crops, but as these will be cleared by the end of September there is an oppor-tunity to plant cabbages which will be ready for cutting the following spring.

Further down the section there is a row of spinach, sown half in February and half in March; each will be cleared in two months and can be followed by lettuces. The next row of lettuces sown in April can again be followed by lettuces sown in June and July, to be used in the early autumn. After this come two double rows of broad beans and two rows of peas; these will be cleared by the end of June or early July and are to be followed by four rows of carrots and two of beetroots for winter use (p. 101).

Section 2 begins with cabbages which have already been planted. There is room for a row of quick-bulbing onions (to be pulled for summer use) before the winter cabbage, which are not planted until July. Before a row of autumn cauliflower there is a catch crop of early white turnips for summer use, sown in April and May. The rest of the section carries the main crops of winter greens for autumn and winter use. These are trans-planted from seeds which can be sown in the middle of the space between the main-crop rows. The transplants will have been pulled up to furnish the main rows, and this method has the advantage of always growing the seed plants on fresh ground.

The first part of section 3 is occupied by main crop potatoes, which, when cleared, are followed by one row of winter spinach and one row of winter lettuces which are cleared in sufficient time to manure and prepare the ground in readiness for runner beans the following season. The two rows of early potatoes are cleared in time to sow two rows of turnips for storing and a row of cabbages to provide plants for the autumn planting referred to in section 1.

Beans, Broad	$\frac{1}{2}$ pt.
Dwarf	$\frac{1}{4}$ pt.
Runner	$\frac{1}{2}$ pt.
Beetroots, round	1 oz.
Broccoli, sprouting	$\frac{1}{16}$ oz.
Brussels sprouts	$\frac{1}{8}$ oz.
Cabbages (autumn sown)	$\frac{1}{16}$ oz.
January King	$\frac{1}{16}$ oz.
Summer	$\frac{1}{16}$ oz.
Carrots (early)	1 oz.
(main crop)	$\frac{1}{2}$ oz.
Cauliflowers (autumn)	$\frac{1}{16}$ oz.
Celery	50 plants
Garden swedes	$\frac{1}{4}$ oz.
Kale, Cottager's	$\frac{1}{16}$ oz.
Hungry Gap	$\frac{1}{8}$ oz.
Leeks	$\frac{1}{4}$ oz.
Lettuces	$\frac{1}{2}$ oz.
Marrows	12 seeds
Onions (autumn sown)	$\frac{1}{2}$ oz.
(spring sown)	$\frac{1}{2}$ oz.
(salads)	$\frac{1}{2}$ oz.
Parsley	$\frac{1}{4}$ oz.
Parsnips	$\frac{1}{2}$ oz.
Peas	$\frac{1}{2}$ pt.
Potatoes (early)	10 lb.
(main crop)	28 lb.
Radishes	1 oz.
Savoys	$\frac{1}{8}$ oz.
Shallots	2 lb.
Spinach beet (summer) (winter)	$\frac{1}{2}$ oz. ea.
Tomatoes	18 plants
Turnips (early) (late)	$\frac{1}{2}$ oz. ea.
Winter cauliflowers (broccoli)	$\frac{1}{16}$ oz.

Pelleted vegetable seeds are now more widely listed in catalogues. The use of this seed allows accurate spacing of seed, also easier thinning and singling resulting in better developed seedlings. Where pelleted seed is sown, it is important to keep the soil thoroughly moist until the seedlings are seen to be emerging above soil level.

1

2

SUCCESSIONAL CROPS: A

1 Harvesting dwarf beans.
2 Removing spent plants.
3 Forking in superphosphate in preparation for next crop.
4 Sowing onions in August to stand the winter.

3

4

1

2

SUCCESSIONAL CROPS: A (*continued*)

1 Sowing lettuces to stand the winter.
2 Showing progress of crops in October.
3 Planting out lettuces in early October.
4 Lettuces ready for cutting in following spring.

3

4

1

2

SUCCESSIONAL CROPS: B

1 Peas ready for picking.
2 Clearing the ground of pea plants.
3 *Left patch:* ground undisturbed for green crops.
   Right patch: preparing ground for carrots and beetroots.
4 Planting savoys 2 feet apart each way on undisturbed ground.

3

4

1

2

SUCCESSIONAL CROPS: B (*continued*)

1 Sowing carrot and beetroot seeds in drills 12 inches apart in July.
2 Progress of crops in October.
3 Showing growth of carrots and beetroots in October.
4 Showing growth of savoys in November.

3

4

1

2

INTERCROPPING
1 Runner Beans, LETTUCES, Peas.
2 Onions, LETTUCES, Tomatoes, Cabbages.
3 Dwarf Beans, LETTUCES, Peas.
4 Leeks, DWARF BEANS, Celery, COS LETTUCES,
   Beetroots.

[103]

3

4

1

2

GREEN MANURING: I

1 Removing spent crop of broad beans.
2 Preparing ground for mustard seeds.
3 Sowing mustard seeds broadcast.
4 Raking over sown ground to cover seeds.

3

4

1

2

GREEN MANURING: 2

1   Mustard crop. Trench opened for digging in.
2   Digging in the mustard crop.
3   Planting cabbages 18 inches between the rows and
     12 inches between the plants, in August.
4   Showing progress of crop in November.

[105]

3

4

irrigating the vegetable garden

by P. RICHARDSON (*National Institute of Agricultural Engineering*)

IRRIGATION IS NOW widely used on market gardens, and there is no doubt that in many areas of this country it is of great benefit. The benefit lies not only in increased yields, and the prevention of crop failure due to drought, but it also makes seed sowing a practical proposition when otherwise the seeds would not germinate through lack of moisture.

THE SOIL WATER

WATER IN THE soil is held by the particles of mineral and organic matter and may also be contained in the spaces between the particles. However, when the spaces are filled with water the soil is water-logged and air is largely excluded. As most vegetable crops will not tolerate a water-logged soil, such water may be harmful unless soil conditions permit it to drain readily to the subsoil and so be removed by drainage.

The water on which the plants draw is that which is held by the soil particles. When the soil contains the maximum amount of water which it can hold, against free drainage, then the soil is said to be at 'field capacity'. At the other end of the scale when the water is so depleted that the plants cannot obtain sufficient water to prevent them from permanently wilting, then the soil is said to be at 'wilting point'.

The amount of water which is required to raise the soil moisture content from wilting point to field capacity will vary from soil to soil. However, as the soil moisture becomes depleted, so the soil tends to hold the remaining water more tightly. For practical purposes, it may be assumed that with moist soils the amount of water available for plant growth is about $1\frac{1}{2}$ in. per foot depth of soil. An inch of water is equivalent to $4\frac{1}{2}$ gallons per square yd. or 140 gallons per square rod.

When water is applied to soil with a deficit, i.e. which is below field capacity, the surface layer is brought to field capacity before water will drain to the next layer. If sufficient water is applied to bring, say, only the top three inches of soil to field capacity, then the water will not penetrate to below this level (unless of course there are cracks or fissures in the soil).

THE LOSS OF WATER FROM THE SOIL

WATER IS LOST from the soil by evaporation from the surface and by transpiration from the leaves of plants. Evaporation from the soil surface takes place at a maximum rate when the surface is wet, but once the surface layer dries out the rate at which water is lost falls to a very low level. In the case of transpiration, i.e. evaporation of water from the leaves of plants, water is lost at a high rate as long as the plants can obtain sufficient water. When the plants can no longer obtain sufficient water to transpire freely, they wilt after which the rate of transpiration drops to a low level.

The actual rate at which water is lost from a plant or from a wet soil surface depends on the amount of energy or heat which is being received from the sun. A large proportion of the sun's energy which falls on plants is used for evaporating water and, as might be expected, the amounts of water which are lost in this way are high.

THE WATER REQUIREMENTS OF PLANTS

BECAUSE THE AMOUNT of water used by the plant in transpiration is so large in comparison to the amount used for other purposes, it is necessary from a practical aspect to consider only the transpiration losses. Obviously if the rate of transpiration is a function of the incoming heat from the sun, then the highest rates of water usage will occur usually in the summer when the temperatures are high and the days are long. Under these conditions as much as 1 in. of water, or $4\frac{1}{2}$ gallons per square yd., may be used in seven to ten days. This assumes of course that the ground is covered by the plants which can obtain sufficient water. Under conditions where the soil surface is dry and a small proportion of the ground only is covered by plants, then proportionally less water will be lost from the soil.

In the south-eastern part of England the average potential water loss is of the order of 18 in. during the growing season. If this is divided into months then the average loss in April is 2 in., May $3\frac{1}{4}$ in., June 4 in., July 4 in., August $3\frac{1}{4}$ in., and September $1\frac{3}{4}$ in. However, some of the loss is made good by natural rainfall and so it is not normally necessary to make good all the water loss by means of irrigation.

Plants can obtain more readily the water which they require from a soil at field capacity than from a soil with a water deficit. Also it has been shown experimentally that higher yields are usually obtained when the soil is maintained at field capacity. It is worth bearing in mind however that, particularly with some crops, the flavour may be reduced when the plants are provided with all the water which they require. With one or two crops it has been shown that there is a critical period when, if the plants are not provided with ample moisture, the yield will be reduced very considerably. Peas are such a crop and the critical period is at the time when they are in flower.

APPLYING IRRIGATION WATER

A COMMON PRACTICE when irrigating gardens is to apply sufficient water to wet the surface of the soil only. This practice is a wasteful one, for much of the water is lost by direct evaporation from the soil surface, and it thus makes little contribution to the water content of the soil below the surface.

In order to be effective it will usually be necessary to apply about 1 in. of water at a time or $4\frac{1}{2}$ gallons of water per square yd. The amount of water applied can be estimated by measuring the quantity of water put out by the irrigation equipment in a certain time (for example, by running the water into a tank or bucket for a known period). Then the area covered by the equipment can be measured and the period required to apply an average of 1 in. of water calculated. A direct method is by placing rain gauges or straight sided, sharp-edged cans (the cans used for the home canning of fruit are suitable and cheap) at different points over the area to be irrigated. After irrigating for a period the depth of water in the cans can be measured. The advantage of this method is that if a reasonable number of cans are used, and are spaced over the area, it will show how evenly the water is being applied as well as the extent of the effective irrigated area. A third method of estimating whether sufficient water has been applied is to use a soil auger and find out to what depth the soil has been wetted. This method has much to commend it because it will show whether the water has restored the soil to field capacity to a sufficient depth. As many plants draw a large part of their water from the first foot of soil, penetration to 9 in. or 12 in. should be aimed at.

1

2

IRRIGATING THE VEGETABLE GARDEN

1   A Square Area Sprinkler in action. The gardener outside the area of the spray shows the regularity of
the area sprayed.
2   A Square Area Sprinkler in action. The spray covers
an area of approximately 40 sq. yds.
3   Perforated Pipe in operation. The metal pipe, 16 feet
long covers an area of 500 square feet.
4   Perforated Hose Pipe watering cabbage seedlings.

3

4

POINTS TO CONSIDER WHEN CHOOSING IRRIGATING EQUIPMENT

IRRIGATION EQUIPMENT should ideally apply the water evenly over the irrigated area and also it should not damage either the soil structure or the plants. We have mentioned previously how the evenness of application can be measured and, as there is little independent information on the performance of the many types of small equipment used in gardens, the trouble of doing this is probably worthwhile.

Damage to the soil structure is caused by the impact of the water droplets breaking the soil crumbs on the surface into smaller particles which are then washed into the pore spaces. The pore spaces thus become reduced and the rate at which water can infiltrate into the soil may be reduced to a fraction of the original rate. When this happens the soil is said to be 'capped'. Large droplets damage the soil structure more readily than small droplets do, particularly in the case of heavy soils which are more readily damaged than are light soils, types of equipment which produce large water droplets should be avoided.

If water is applied at too fast a rate to a soil, then local flooding may take place and damage to the soil structure may result. Plants may be damaged also through either being beaten down by the irrigation water or by the soil being washed away from the plants.

The size of the drops of water is a function of the water pressure and of the size of the orifice, the higher pressures and the smaller orifices producing smaller droplets. The droplet size is not easily measured without the appropriate equipment but a visual assessment of the soil surface after irrigating will give a good indication of the suitability of the equipment. The distance which the water is thrown is also an indication as the greater the length of throw the larger is the droplet size. If the soil becomes badly capped then the equipment is not suitable for the prevailing conditions.

THE WATER SUPPLY

MOST GARDENS WILL use water from the domestic mains. The important factors to consider are the pressure and the discharge rate or water output. It is not generally realized that as the discharge rate is increased so the pressure drops. This is because the supply pipe is of limited size and as the flow increases so the friction loss is increased.

Where the water supply is some considerable distance from the vegetable garden then a very long hose must be used. In order to avoid an undue loss of pressure the hose should be of sufficiently large diameter, and often it is worthwhile to use a $\frac{3}{4}$ in. hose even though the supply is from a $\frac{1}{2}$ in. tap. If possible it is better to have the supply laid on to the vegetable garden and with thick walled polythene pipe, this is now a comparatively simple job.

THE IRRIGATION EQUIPMENT

SEVERAL TYPES OF equipment are available and the selection of the best type to use depends on the pressure and discharge rate of the water supply, the type of soil, the garden layout, and also the cost.

ROTARY SPRINKLERS

ONLY THE SMALLEST types are suitable for gardens of limited area and they all have the disadvantage of watering circular areas. This means that it will be difficult to water all the garden evenly, and there will be small areas which get either too little or too much water.

The importance of choosing a sprinkler equipped with nozzles which are small enough to break the water into small droplets cannot be over-stressed.

Some of the reaction types of sprinkler tend to apply most of the water on the outer part of the circle covered and the area near to the sprinkler receives insufficient water. One sort in which the sprinkler head rotates rapidly does appear to avoid this pitfall. The small hammer types of sprinkler should be quite suitable if the area is not too small, and the better sorts do distribute the water reasonably evenly.

SQUARE AREA SPRINKLERS

BECAUSE MOST VEGETABLE gardens are rectangular, this type of sprinkler has obvious advantages. They are much more expensive, however, than most other types. Because they are equipped with a number of nozzles, the total discharge rate is fairly high, and if a small supply pipe is used the pressure loss may be unduly high. Like the rotary sprinklers they only require moving every two or three hours.

SINGLE SPRAY NOZZLE

GARDEN HOSES ARE often sold complete with a single nozzle which can be adjusted to give a fine or a coarse spray (large or small droplets). The normal method of use is to fix them to the handle of a fork and set them to water a narrow strip of garden. When one strip has been watered it is moved to the next strip and so on. The main advantage of the method is that it is cheap. The disadvantages are that it requires moving frequently (as do most stationary devices) and that the water is applied rather unevenly. However, in a very small garden it may be possible to operate one of these whereas some of the other devices will be too large.

PERFORATED HOSE PIPE

THE PERFORATED HOSE pipe is roughly the garden equivalent of the oscillated sprayline. However, in order to water a fairly wide area it has a number of holes in each section where the oscillated sprayline has only one. As the water jets are stationary water is applied to the soil at a high rate and unless the soil has a high infiltration rate (such as an open sandy soil) local flooding is liable to occur. The equipment will require moving fairly frequently, perhaps every $\frac{1}{2}$–$\frac{3}{4}$ hour. The evenness of distribution of the water is affected adversely if the hose twists a little so a hose of fairly stiff material is best for the purpose. The length of perforated hose which can be operated satisfactorily depends on the size of the supply pipe, the supply pressure and the size of the hose. An operating pressure of 40–60 lb./sq. in. is desirable and the maximum pressure drop between the first and the last orifice should be not more than about 15 per cent of the supply pressure. With a $\frac{1}{2}$ in. hose pipe the number of orifices which can be operated satisfactorily may be about 25 to 30, although with a poor mains supply it may be almost half this number.

TRICKLE IRRIGATION

ALTHOUGH TRICKLE IRRIGATION has a number of advantages it is generally too expensive to be considered for the vegetable garden. It is expensive because it applies water very slowly, and therefore a lot of equipment is required if all the vegetable garden is to be given sufficient water. One of the cheapest methods is to use perforated lay-flat polythene tubing.

machinery in the vegetable garden

by J. S. WOLFE (*National Institute of Agricultural Engineering*)

ONE OF THE heaviest and slowest tasks in the vegetable garden is digging the soil to prepare it for planting or sowing the crops. Hoeing to keep down weeds and the soil surface open also takes a lot of time. A suitably selected motor cultivator can greatly help the gardener in these jobs. The main advantage of these machines is that they enable the work to be done faster. The busy gardener is thus able to complete a job in the limited and scattered periods he can devote to his garden, or when weather and soil conditions are favourable. Motor cultivators can also in most cases reduce the physical effort required of the gardener in doing these jobs; but in some circumstances he may have to work as hard as if he were doing the job by hand, though for a shorter time!

Reliability is one of the most important features required in a motor cultivator. If it fails to start or essential parts wear or break it is not available when required and the gardener is then forced to do by hand work whose scale has become adjusted to machine operation. If he does his own repairs he must find the time for this as well as cultivation by hand in the meantime. Two-stroke engines are the most common offenders for faulty starting, but if simple maintenance is carried out before and after use, this trouble can be avoided. Regular overall maintenance and checking for worn, loose or broken parts also avoids much delay and the expense of repairs or replacements.

Almost all cultivators whose size and price is suitable for all but very large gardens, work the soil by means of a rotary tiller. This consists of a number of tools which revolve about a transverse horizontal axis, driven by the engine. Various types of tools are available for different kinds of work. Hoe blades are most common as standard equipment, and are used for general tillage and mixing-in light cover crops or dressings of manure, and for hoeing the surface soil to destroy weeds or break a crust. Curved hoe blades are bent over on a gentler curve than the right-angle bend of the common hoe blade. They are said to be better for mixing-in cover crops as a mulch, and for digging when the soil is wet, or in heavy soils, but not suitable for preparing seed-beds. Finger tines are supplied for one machine, for stirring the soil to prepare a seed-bed without excessive pulverization. Slasher blades, which are curved both from side to side and backwards from root to tip, are provided for several models, for cutting long cover crops and partially mixing them with the soil. Knife tines, which lie in one plane and are either straight or curved forwards or backwards from the root, are for vertical slicing of matted grass or weeds either to enable them to be mixed into the soil by another type of tine or blade, or just to invigorate old grass which has become too matted. Pick tines, which curve forwards from root to tip and end in either a pick or a chisel point, are for breaking-up hard soil which blades will not do so well. They also mix-in cover crops which are already cut into short pieces, or well rotted manure. Finally, a few machines can be provided with disks arranged part-spirally, which are for making furrows or ridges in loose soil, or for scraping the surface of the soil or of paths and drives to remove weeds. The rotary tiller can be removed from practically all motor cultivators, and devices for doing many other jobs in the garden attached in its place or in some other way so that the power of the engine can be used to operate them. Grass cutters, lawn mowers and hedge trimmers are the most common, but sprayers, saws and transport barrows are often supplied, and, for the larger machines, ploughs and other draught implements.

Motor cultivators are of three main types, differing in their complexity (and flexibility), weight and price. The simplest type has the rotary tiller in front of the engine and directly coupled to it, with no clutch or provision for changing the speed of rotation other than by the throttle control of the engine. Wheels are provided to support the weight of the machine when it is being transported from place to place and usually when it is in work, and handles to enable the operator to guide and control it. The wheels are not driven by the engine: traction is provided either by the rotary tiller when it is in work or by the operator pushing or pulling on the handles. The different models range in power from $\frac{3}{4}$ to 3 h.p., and in weight from 50 to 100 lb. approximately. The standard width of the tiller is 10–18 in., but the tools are usually pre-assembled in 'disks' or sections so that by the addition or removal of sections the width may be increased to 18, 20 or even 24 in. for lighter work, or decreased to 7 or 8 in. for heavier work. In easy conditions, machines of this type will work in the forward direction, that is with the tiller in front and the operator behind. It is necessary to swing the tiller from side to side to avoid leaving the soil unworked in the middle, where the shaft or chain drive requires a gap between the tools. If the soil is hard, however, the tiller tools will not penetrate very deeply, and the machine will tend to travel forward at a fairly high speed unless the operator pulls back on the handles. In these circumstances, and in any case to obtain a working depth greater than about 4 in., backward working with an open trench is necessary. This is possible by turning round the tiller head so that it rotates in a direction tending to propel the machine towards the operator. The operator can then, after a little practice, lift the handles so that the full weight of the machine rests on the tiller, at the same time bracing himself against the handles so that the machine does not 'charge' at him. The tiller will then dig deeply into the soil in one place, throwing the dislodged soil away from it. When the tiller has dug down to the required depth, the machine is rested on its wheels and the tiller is levered to the side by means of the handles, so that the hole is extended sideways to form a trench. When the required width (or length) of trench is formed, the work proceeds backwards towards the operator by cutting away the wall of the trench a little bit at a time across its full width (or length).

Going up the scale, the next type has the tiller underneath the engine so that most of the weight of the machine rests on it to assist penetration when necessary. A clutch of some form is provided in almost all models to enable the drive to the tiller to be disconnected by the operator. Some models are provided with means of changing the speed of the tiller beyond the range possible by using the engine throttle control. Nearly all models are provided with two non-driven wheels at the back to support the weight when the machine is being transported from place to place. In the lower-powered (and lighter) models ($1\frac{3}{4}$–2 or $2\frac{1}{4}$ h.p. range) the wheels are used as in the smaller type of machine, but are adjustable for height which provides a measure of regulation of the depth of working. In the higher-powered models ($2\frac{1}{2}$–4 h.p. range) these wheels can be lifted right off the ground, and control of the depth of working and speed of travel is effected by means of a single tine at the rear whose use will be explained presently. Weight figures are given in very few of the manufacturers' leaflets, but one model weighs as little as 55 lb., and weights may be assumed to extend to about 150 lb. or perhaps slightly more. As in the lighter type, the standard tiller width (10–15 in.) may be increased or decreased by the addition or removal of pre-assembled tool sections. Except for one model whose tiller can be turned round to enable it to be used for backward digging, this type works in the forward direction. Traction is provided by the tiller. Travel speed is controlled by the

1

2

MACHINERY IN THE VEGETABLE GARDEN

1 A Rotary Tiller mixing in a cover crop.
2 A Rotary Tiller being used for deep digging.
3 A Rotary Tiller producing a coarse tilth.
4 A Rotary Tiller being used for a fine tilth.

3

4

operator applying pressure downwards on the handles so that more of the weight of the machine is transferred to the tine at the rear. This reduces the speed. By lifting the handles to reduce the weight on the rear tine, the speed is increased. Alteration of travel speed has some effect on the fineness of the tilth produced by the tiller. Slower travel tends to result in a fine, perhaps powdery tilth, and faster travel in a coarser tilth. Speed of rotation of the tiller also tends to affect the fineness of the tilth produced, higher speeds resulting in finer tilth. Depth of working is regulated by adjusting the height of the rear tine: raising it allows the tiller to work deeper. In the higher-powered models of this type of cultivator, traction wheels can be fitted in place of the tillage-tool sections on the tiller shaft to convert the machine to a tractor.

The next step up the scale of advancing complexity of machines brings one into the realm of true tractors, i.e. of machines in which the engine drives the wheels in addition to the tiller or other attachments. Those of interest to the gardener have a power range of $1\frac{1}{2}$–4 h.p. approximately, and their weights range from about 100 lb. to nearly 300 lb. The standard width of the rotary tiller is 10–14 in., but an alternative wider tiller can be obtained with some models. Extension of the tiller width by the addition of tools or tool assemblies is usually not possible. A clutch is always provided, and usually means of changing the speed of the drives to the wheels and the implement, either together or separately. These machines are easiest to control of the three types described, since the travel speed is regulated by the gear selected and the setting of the engine throttle. The depth of working of the rotary tiller is regulated by the setting of a skid behind the tiller which may be either on an adjustable stalk or incorporated in the hinged rear part of a hood covering the tiller. Thus when the machine is working, the operator merely has to steer it by means of the handles. A point worth noting in connection with the steerage of both this and the other types of machine when hoeing between rows of crops is that accurate steerage close to the rows is best achieved by working as close as possible to the row on one side, on one pass along the strip between the rows, and to the row on the other side on the return pass.

A motor Cultivator showing details of the motor and hoe blades.

A Rotary Tiller showing details of the motor and tines.

Generally, gardening by machine requires a different approach from that when manual methods are used, particularly in the arrangement of the crop rows. To avoid a disproportionate amount of unproductive time due to turning the machine at the ends of the rows, especially in hoeing, the rows should be at least 30 ft. long, or longer if the size of the garden will allow it. If this length of row means that too much of particular crops would be grown, half-rows of crops not in great demand which have approximately the same lengths of growing season could be put end-to-end. It is important also to space the rows sufficiently widely to allow room for the machine to pass between them when the plants are fully grown. One way of doing this is to make the distance of any row from its neighbour the width of the machine plus half the spread of the plants in one row when fully grown plus half the spread of the plants in the next row when fully grown. In this system the rows of successive crops will seldom come in the same places because of the differing spreads of the crops and numbers of rows of each required. Hence the whole of the cropped area must be tilled as deeply as is considered necessary to ensure good growth for all crops. Because the rows are more widely spaced than in a garden worked by hand, a larger area must be tilled to full depth. This is of no great consequence when a mechanical tiller is used.

There is another system which avoids tilling the whole area to the maximum depth. This involves keeping to permanent positions for the rows. At each position a strip or bed twice the width of the cultivator is tilled to the maximum depth required for the crops, and as many crop rows are fitted in each bed as will fill the width of the bed when the crops are fully grown. A space equal to the width of the cultivator is left between the beds which is tilled shallowly to keep down the weeds. In this system there may be two, or even three, rows of the smaller crops in a bed, and surface cultivation between these rows has to be done by hand tools as most motor cultivators are too wide to go between them. The plants soon spread over the whole bed, and smother the weeds so that hoeing is not needed in the bed after a few weeks. The spaces between the beds are always wide enough for the motor cultivator to pass along them. Two, or even three, passes may be required to work the full width when the crops are young. Even when they are fully grown the cultivator can still pass between the beds for weed-control cultivations, or for spraying or dusting when suitable appliances are fitted to the machine.

It is essential when laying out a garden for mechanical cultivation to leave a wide enough space between the ends of the rows and a hedge or fence. There must be sufficient space to turn the machine round in order if necessary to work back along the strip just worked. The minimum width of this path or headland should be equal to the distance from the front of the machine to the operator's heel when he is holding the handles and puts one leg a pace backwards. For turning in more comfort, a width of about twice the length of the machine may be required. This turning area may be kept free of weeds by shallow cultivations, or it may be sown with grass which is kept cut short by means of the grass cutting attachment available for many of these motor cultivators.

MACHINERY IN THE VEGETABLE GARDEN

1   A Rotary Tiller adapted to make ridges.
2   Surface cultivation between rows of a Brassica crop.
3   Surface cultivation between crops spaced closely together.

1

2

3

REMINDERS FOR JANUARY

GATHER brussels sprouts and spinach beet.

CUT winter cabbages and savoys.

LIFT Jerusalem artichokes, celery, leeks and parsnips as required for use.

USE FROM STORE beetroots, carrots, marrows, potatoes, onions, shallots, swedes and turnips.

PLAN the year's cropping of the vegetable garden.

ORDER vegetable seeds and potato 'seed'.

SOW onion Ailsa Craig and cauliflower Snowball under glass. Sow broad beans, carrot Amsterdam Forcing, lettuces, peas and radishes in cloches and frames.

PLANT lettuces in cloches and frames (see pp. 83 and 85).

DRESS the plot intended for green crops (cabbages, etc.); should the ground require lime, apply 20 lb. of ground chalk or limestone or 15 lb. of hydrated lime to the surface of each square rod after digging has been completed. Ground intended for green crops to over-winter should not be disturbed; clear any spent crops or weeds, apply lime to the surface of the soil and hoe in to prevent loss by wind.

Savoy Ormskirk Late Green.

Cabbage January King.

REMINDERS FOR FEBRUARY

GATHER brussels sprouts, kales and spinach beet.

CUT savoys.

LIFT Jerusalem artichokes, celery, leeks and parsnips as required for use.

USE FROM STORE beetroots, carrots, onions, shallots, swedes and turnips.

SOW lettuces, onions, radishes and summer cabbages (for transplanting in the open) in cloches and frames. Sow broad beans and round-seeded spinach in the open at the end of the month.

PLANT Jerusalem artichokes and shallots.

LIFT parsnips to check growth and store under protective material at the north side of a wall or fence if possible.

ARRANGE 'seed' potatoes in trays, rose end uppermost, to sprout and place in a frost-proof, *light* and airy structure to encourage short sturdy sprouts in readiness for planting in April.

RUB OFF any sprouts as they develop on eating potatoes in store.

DRESS the ground intended for roots with a mixture of 3 lb. of superphosphate, $1\frac{1}{2}$ lb. of sulphate of potash and $\frac{3}{4}$ lb. of sulphate of ammonia to a rod of ground; apply to the surface of the ground and hoe in about two weeks before sowing a crop.

Garden Swedes.

REMINDERS FOR MARCH

GATHER brussels sprouts, spinach beet and spring greens.

CUT brussels sprout tops, savoys and turnip tops.

LIFT leeks and Jerusalem artichokes for use as required.

USE FROM STORE beetroots, carrots, onions, turnips and swedes.

SUCCESSIONAL SOWINGS. Broad beans and spinach.

SOW brussels sprouts, cabbages, celery (trench and self-blanching), lettuces, leeks, onions, parsley, parsnips, peas and radishes.

PLANT August-sown onions, onion sets and lettuces which have been raised in cloches and frames.

LIFT remaining crop of leeks to check growth and 'heel-in' in a shady spot, if possible.

HOE, using the Dutch hoe, freely between all growing crops and vacant ground on every favourable occasion; endeavour to move all ground at least every ten days when growth is active to retain moisture and keep down weeds.

APPLY a dressing of sulphate of ammonia or nitrate of soda to spring cabbages, lettuces and spinach at the rate of 1 oz. per yard run, and hoe in thoroughly.

MOUND up asparagus beds if the soil is light and apply a general fertilizer.

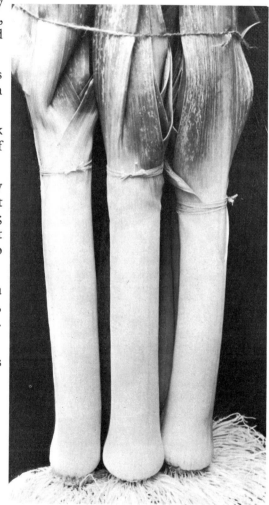

Well-grown specimens of Leek Prizetaker.

REMINDERS FOR APRIL

GATHER brussels sprout shoots, sprouting broccoli, kales, spring greens and turnip tops.

CUT asparagus, lettuces which were planted in cloches and frames during December and January and spring cabbages.

PULL radishes.

LIFT leeks from heeling-in ground as required for use.

USE FROM STORE beetroots, carrots, onions, swedes and turnips.

SOW beetroots, cabbages, carrots, cauliflowers, dwarf and runner beans (in cloches and frames), onions for pickling, onions for salads, sweet corn (in cloches and frames), tomatoes (under glass) and turnips.

SUCCESSIONAL SOWINGS. Lettuces, peas, radishes and spinach.

PLANT globe artichokes, cauliflowers, onions (raised under glass), onion sets and potatoes, both early and maincrop.

THIN spinach.

STAKE peas.

HOE between all crops.

REMOVE all cabbage and brussels sprout stumps and stack loosely to dry before burning, to reduce cabbage aphis attacks.

PREPARE a trench 15 inches wide at the end of the month as soon as the ground is free for a double row of celery.

APPLY 2 lb. of mixed fertilizer (2 parts of superphosphate, 1 part of sulphate of potash and 1 part of sulphate of ammonia) per 30 feet of potato drill at planting time. On the plot intended for green crops apply a mixture of 3 lb. of super-phosphate and 2 lb. of sulphate of potash per rod. Hoe the dressing thoroughly into the surface of the ground.

Well-grown Kale plant.

REMINDERS FOR MAY

GATHER spinach and sprouting broccoli.

CUT asparagus, cabbages and lettuces.

LIFT leeks from heeling-in ground as required.

USE FROM STORE onions.

PULL radishes and onions for salads.

SOW French and runner beans, kales, savoys, sweet corn and winter cabbages. Last week: marrows and ridge cucumbers.

SUCCESSIONAL SOWINGS. Beetroots, carrots, lettuces, radishes and turnips.

PLANT brussels sprouts and potatoes (late) early in the month, and tomatoes (in cloches and frames).

THIN beetroots, carrots, lettuces, onions, parsnips and turnips.

STAKE peas and runner beans.

DRAW a little soil over potato shoots as they appear through the soil should frost threaten.

EARTH early potatoes.

MULCH where possible such crops as beans, peas, etc.

HOE between all crops.

COLLECT all waste vegetable matter, coarse grass, lawn clippings, annual weeds—in fact anything from the garden that will rot down for the compost heap. Continue to collect all material as it comes to hand right through the year.

APPLY if necessary a dressing of nitrate of soda or sulphate of ammonia to such crops as early cauliflowers, lettuces and spinach.

DIG ground recently cleared of a late green crop and prepare for leeks.

WATCH for blackfly attacking broad beans, carrot fly, onion fly, cabbage-root maggot and turnip flea beetle, and apply insecticides if necessary (see relevant sections of text pp. 36–49).

REMINDERS FOR JUNE

GATHER broad beans, peas and spinach.

CUT cabbages, cauliflowers and lettuces. Finish cutting asparagus about the second or third week of the month.

PULL radishes and onions for salads.

SOW garden swedes.

SUCCESSIONAL SOWINGS. Beetroots, carrots, lettuces, runner beans and turnips.

PLANT brussels sprouts, early cabbages, cauliflowers, celery, marrows, self-blanching celery and tomatoes.

THIN beetroots, carrots, lettuces and turnips.

STAKE runner beans, tie tomatoes.

PINCH OUT tops of broad beans when in full flower.

HOE between all crops.

APPLY a dressing of nitrate of soda or sulphate of ammonia, 1 oz. per square yard, to such crops as beetroots, carrots, onions and parsnips after thinning the crops. Carrots and onions, when attacked by fly, benefit considerably by such an application. Spray celery against celery fly (see p. 78).

WATCH for blackfly on broad beans, cabbage-root maggot, carrot fly, celery-leaf maggot and onion fly, and apply insecticides if necessary (see pp. 36–49).

Well-grown Cos Lettuce.

Well-grown Cabbage Lettuce.

REMINDERS FOR JULY

GATHER dwarf and runner beans and peas.

CUT cabbages, cauliflowers, globe artichokes and lettuces.

PULL early beetroots, carrots, green onions and early turnips as required for use.

LIFT early potatoes as required for use.

SOW cabbages for spring cutting (last week) in the north only, spinach beet, also kale Hungry Gap and parsley.

SUCCESSIONAL SOWINGS. Beetroots, carrots, lettuces and turnips for storing.

PLANT late cauliflowers, winter cabbages, leeks, sprouting broccoli, kales and savoys.

THIN beetroots, carrots, lettuces and garden swedes.

WATER celery, globe artichokes, marrows and runner beans when necessary.

EARTH brussels sprouts.

TIE tomatoes and remove side growths as they develop.

PROTECT cauliflower curds from the sun with leaves broken from the plant.

FEED celery with a little sulphate of ammonia or nitrate of soda. Dust with soot.

HARVEST shallots.

PINCH OUT the growing points of runner bean plants when they have reached the top of their poles.

SPRAY maincrop potatoes with maneb or zineb (first week) and celery with Bordeaux mixture or zineb at three-weekly intervals until the end of September.

HOE between all crops.

REMINDERS FOR AUGUST

GATHER dwarf and runner beans, sweet corn, tomatoes, and herbs for drying.

CUT cauliflowers, globe artichokes, lettuces, marrows and ridge cucumbers.

PULL beetroots, carrots, onions and turnips as required for use.

LIFT early potatoes as required for use.

SOW cabbages for spring use (first and second week), lettuces (to be transplanted in cloches or frames for late autumn and winter use), onions for spring planting, onions for spring salads and winter spinach.

PLANT the latest green crops as early as possible in the month in order to fill up all the ground allotted to these important winter vegetables.

THIN beetroots, carrots, July-sown kales, parsley and spinach beet.

EARTH kales and winter cauliflowers.

BEND DOWN tops of August-sown onions that have stood the winter and are now completing their growth and lift about a fortnight later, exposing the roots to the full sun.

WATER celery, marrows and runner beans when necessary.

STOP tomato plants when four trusses of fruits have set.

PROTECT cauliflower curds with leaves broken from the plant.

SPRAY celery with Bordeaux mixture or zineb against leaf spot and outdoor tomatoes with a liquid copper spray, maneb or zineb to control blight.

HOE between all crops.

Tomato Harbinger bearing heavy crop of fruits.

REMINDERS FOR SEPTEMBER

GATHER runner beans, sweet corn and tomatoes.

CUT cabbages, cauliflowers, globe artichokes, lettuces, marrows and ridge cucumbers.

PULL beetroots, carrots and turnips as required for use.

LIFT potatoes for immediate use and for storing when ready and self-blanching celery.

HARVEST onions and ripe marrows before the end of the month.

SOW winter lettuces, winter spinach and turnips for turnip tops.

PLANT cabbages for spring cutting and lettuces in cloches and frames for late autumn and winter use.

THIN winter spinach, and turnips for storing.

BEND DOWN tops of spring-sown onions on completing their growth and lift about a fortnight later, exposing the roots to the full sun.

PROTECT cauliflower curds with leaves broken from the plant.

WATER celery, marrows and runner beans when necessary.

SPRAY celery with Bordeaux mixture or zineb and outdoor tomatoes with liquid copper, maneb or zineb.

REMOVE suckers at the base of celery plants, tie the plants and thoroughly soak the trench before earthing for the first time.

PULL UP tomato plants at the end of the month with green fruits attached; transfer to a suitable place under cover to finish ripening. Alternatively remove green fruits which should be wrapped in paper and placed in a cupboard or drawer to ripen or protect late fruits with cloches or lights.

TRIM OFF the largest leaves of the March-sown parsley in order to encourage a fresh crop of young leaves for the winter.

HOE between all crops.

CUT OFF and burn potato tops should these be badly infected with disease.

LIFT potatoes early in the month on ground where wireworm is troublesome.

WATCH for cabbage caterpillars and celery-leaf maggot.

REMINDERS FOR OCTOBER

GATHER brussels sprouts, the last runner beans, spinach beet and outside leaves of winter spinach and lettuces grown in cloches and frames from a sowing made in August.

CUT cabbage, cauliflowers and lettuces.

LIFT self-blanching celery and potatoes for storing.

LIFT AND STORE beetroots, carrots sown before July, and turnips for storing only.

SOW lettuces in cloches and frames between October 10th and 20th.

PLANT cabbages for spring cutting, and winter lettuces from the seed rows before the middle of the month, if possible.

THIN winter lettuces in the seed rows to 3 inches apart.

EARTH celery (second time) and leeks.

BLANCH endive by covering with darkened cloches or frames.

PROTECT late cauliflowers from frost injury by leaves broken from the plant.

TIE onions into ropes and hang in a suitable storing place as soon as the bulbs are thoroughly ripened.

DOUBLE DIG any grassland on which it is proposed to grow vegetables during the coming season. No manure should be necessary at the time of digging (see p. 14).

HOE, if possible, between all crops, especially spring cabbages, winter onions, lettuces and spinach, to stand the winter.

REMOVE all spent crops immediately, especially the stumps of cabbages, cauliflowers, etc.; stumps of green crops should be dug up and dried before consigning them to the bonfire. In this way attacks of cabbage-root gall may be minimized.

CUT down asparagus plants to near ground level and mound up the row if the soil is heavy.

Turnip New Model.

REMINDERS FOR NOVEMBER

GATHER brussels sprouts and spinach beet.

CUT cabbages, cauliflowers and lettuces grown in cloches and frames from a sowing made in August.

LIFT celery, leeks and parsnips as required for use.

USE FROM STORE beetroots, carrots, marrows, onions, shallots, potatoes and turnips.

LIFT AND STORE beetroots (July sown) and turnips.

EARTH celery finally.

PRICK OUT lettuces sown in October into further cloches or frames, spacing the seedlings 2 inches square.

PROTECT late cauliflowers from frost.

REMOVE yellow leaves from brussels sprout plants and other green crops and put them on the compost heap. Remove dead and decaying leaves and stems from globe artichokes.

CLEAR all runner bean haulms for the compost heap.

TAKE UP AND STORE stakes used for runner beans and tomatoes.

DOUBLE DIG at least one-third of the vegetable garden as the ground is cleared of crops such as potatoes and roots and, if possible, give this portion a good dressing of farmyard manure or compost. This portion should be suitable for growing those crops marked section 1 on the plan, during the next year.

Cabbage Baby Roundhead.

Cabbage Winnigstadt.

REMINDERS FOR DECEMBER

GATHER brussels sprouts and spinach beet.

CUT winter cabbages and savoys.

LIFT Jerusalem artichokes, celery, leeks and parsnips as required for use.

LIFT AND STORE carrots (July sown) and garden swedes.

USE FROM STORE beetroots, carrots, marrows, potatoes, onions, shallots and turnips.

EXAMINE onions, potatoes and other roots in store, taking out decayed specimens. Repeat in January, February and March.

PLANT lettuces into cloches or frames $8\frac{1}{2}$ inches square (see pp. 83 and 85). The seed for this planting was sown in October and the lettuces should be fit for use during April.

PROTECT celery and globe artichokes with straw or bracken and increase the protective material of outdoor clamps and potatoes in store, should severe frost threaten.

HEEL OVER winter cauliflower (broccoli).

DIG all ground deeply as it becomes vacant. The importance of early digging cannot be stressed too strongly and, should time permit, the ground intended for roots can with advantage be double dug, but no fertilizer should be added until the spring (see February notes).

Well-grown Celery.